C000245857

The Secrets *to* No-Fail Baking *with* Epic Results

The SOURDOUGH *Whisperer*

Elaine Boddy

Author of *Whole Grain Sourdough at Home*

PAGE STREET
PUBLISHING CO.

PAGE STREET
PUBLISHING CO.

Copyright © 2022 Elaine Boddy

First published in 2022 by
Page Street Publishing Co.
27 Congress Street, Suite 1511
Salem, MA 01970
www.pagestreetpublishing.com

All rights reserved. No part of this book may be reproduced or used, in any form
or by any means, electronic or mechanical, without prior permission in writing
from the publisher.

Distributed by Macmillan, sales in Canada by The Canadian Manda Group.

26   25   24   23   22   3   4   5

ISBN-13: 978-1-64567-484-9
ISBN-10: 1-64567-484-3

Library of Congress Control Number: 2021937939

Cover and book design by Page Street Publishing Co.
Photography by James Kennedy

Printed and bound in the United States

Page Street Publishing protects our planet by donating to nonprofits
like The Trustees, which focuses on local land conservation.

With the greatest love and
thanks always to my special boys,
Graham, Ben and Bob

xxx

Contents

Part 2
The Recipes   69

Dearest reader,

When I was writing this book, the U.K. was still in lockdown as a result of the global COVID-19 pandemic. During the uncertain times that we all lived through, sourdough was a shining light for so many people, and it was my joy and pleasure to be able to assist people all over the world on their sourdough journeys and see it bring so much happiness and excitement in the midst of the crisis.

I believe that sourdough had such huge popularity through it all partly because, suddenly, people had time on their hands while being stuck at home and were finally able to try making sourdough. This was partly because people had seen others making it and wanted to join in, and partly because of people wanting to share their love of sourdough, many creating online family and friend groups for their bread making. It was a delight and something exciting and fun to do. For me, and many of the sourdough bakers that I conversed with over that time, sourdough also provided a consistent, mindful, positive influence, a reminder that life goes on and that nature continues; as we fed our starters and watched them grow and respond, it was a sign of positivity and growth that was much needed.

This wonderful thing called sourdough often raises questions though—often the same questions time and again—and it is these queries and their answers that form so much of what I am sharing in this book, as they show me exactly what home bakers worry about when making sourdough. There is something about sourdough that can seem complicated or confusing when it truly is simple. The aim of everything that I write and share is to show that true simplicity and to provide you with the confidence and clarity to be able to make sourdough successfully in your own home, week after week. I have worked hard to download everything possible that I can from my sourdough brain to provide you with all of the hints and tips and answers that you may ever need.

Making sourdough can be for life, not just for a pandemic or a passing phase. This can be the bread that you make on a regular basis for your household. Once you start making sourdough, and get into a routine of making it, it can continue on for as long as you enjoy the bread.

This book will show you that you can plan and control your sourdough making; it does not need to control you. I hope it provides a sense of freedom to relax and enjoy the process. You will also see how to convert the recipes to make doughs of any size, bake them in various ways and really find what works best for you as you make sourdough for your home. This book will show you that sourdough is truly versatile and endlessly forgiving. I am often called "The Sourdough Whisperer" and my hope is that with this book, you will become your very own Sourdough Whisperer, literally speaking to your amazing starter, nurturing its powers, reading its moods and behavior and therefore understanding how to manage your starter and your doughs to fit in with your life.

My promise, always, to all of my readers and foodbod bakers, is that you will not find any jargon, percentages, unknown terminology, overcomplicated processes or unnecessary steps in this book—or in any of my recipes; my focus is always on user-friendly, simple steps. I hope you find these directions and tips helpful and that you enjoy all the recipes that follow on.

Happy baking!

With love and flour,

Elaine
x   x

Part 1

YOUR ULTIMATE GUIDE TO MAKING SOURDOUGH

A standard sourdough bread dough is comprised of just four elements:

Starter, flour, water and salt.

As you know, each of these elements plays a key part in the success of the dough. Each of these elements can also lead to dough not behaving as you expected, which is why it is important to understand each of their roles, how they affect dough and how they can be tweaked to enhance doughs—about all of which you will find lots of information and tips throughout this section and the book at large.

But there is also a fifth element that is often missed from recipes:

Temperature.

In fact, the temperature of your kitchen is possibly the most important element to understand, which is why you will see room temperature mentioned so often in this book and in everything sourdough-based that I share.

If there is one gift I try to give to new sourdough bakers, it is to understand the effects of temperature on your dough. Colder temperatures slow down every part of the process and warmer temperatures speed it up, and both can affect the outcome of your baked loaves. This is something that took me a couple of years to fully comprehend and that I am now so happy that I can share with others. Of all of the key items that will help your sourdough journey, a room thermometer is the one I would recommend. I use a thermometer that measures the lowest and highest temperature across the previous 24 hours, and it is vital to my dough success.

Being aware of the temperature in your kitchen, plus temperature changes throughout the year, will help you fully understand how your starter and dough behave, how to plan your dough making and how to control it. Making dough is only one part of making sourdough; understanding how it behaves and why is the path to your sourdough success, and in this section, I will show you how to apply this understanding while keeping the process simple and straightforward.

ALL ABOUT STARTER

Sourdough starter is the key to it all. It is the live yeast in our doughs; it is what gives sourdough bread its flavor, looks and distinctiveness. It is the magic element in sourdough making. I love my starter. It brings me great joy and does a perfect job for me each time I use it. It is my second child!

But all that romanticism aside, the fact is, sourdough starter is a living element created by fermenting flour and water until it creates a thick, luscious paste full of life and activity. The natural wild yeast found in the flour, which also attracts wild yeast that is naturally in the air all around us, produces bubbles and growth and the power needed to lift doughs.

To strip it down to the absolute basics, sourdough starter is the leavening agent in our bread. It is what gives the dough growth and lift, and then produces the rise in the baked goods. The key difference between starter and other leavening agents is that starter is in liquid form and lives and lasts forever, as opposed to other raising agents, such as commercially sold yeast or baking powder, which are in dried form and can be added straight from a package.

Sourdough starter is different only in that it is constant; it remains as a living element in the fridge, asleep until we want to use it. When we want to make dough, we take it from the fridge, we feed it and we then leave it to digest that food of flour and water and to become active and lively. Once that happens, we remove what we need for our dough and return the remaining starter back to the fridge to go back to sleep until we next want to use it. Other than when making a new starter, using and maintaining a sourdough starter can be as simple as that. It does not need daily attention or daily feeding and using; it can be left dormant in the cold of the fridge until it is needed.

Feeding a starter is often termed *refreshing*. Before feeding, your starter will have been sleeping, so think of feeding it as waking it up from its slumber and giving it breakfast. That way we give it its nutrition and energy, just as we would for ourselves. When we wake up, we need food and nourishment to give us energy to do whatever lies ahead in our day; our starter is exactly the same.

But we also need to grow extra starter for each use; otherwise, we would very quickly use up our stored starter and have none left. Hence, feeding refreshes and replenishes our starters.

What Makes All Starters Different and Why

Like all living beings, every starter is different. They look different, smell different and behave differently. This is due to several factors: the flour used in your starter, the water, the environment, where you live and how you use your starter.

Each of these elements will produce a different color, but also behavior, smell and flavor in your starter. The wild yeast naturally found in flour will be different in every type of flour, plus different flours bring their own characteristics. Even two white flours can produce two very individual starters. When you factor in your water, the wild yeast naturally floating in the air around your kitchen, as well as the temperature of your kitchen, it all adds up to make your starter truly individual.

For example, my starter smells like paint (it is a very active, successful starter; it just happens to smell like paint). I could bring my starter to your home, and over time that smell would change from being fed with your flour and water and living in your environment. This would change the flavor and behavior, too.

Likewise with looks, starters made with white flours tend to be bubbly; starters made with whole-grain flours are not. Bubbles are very fulfilling to see in your starter, but if yours does not bubble, it does not mean it is defective. It is growth and activity that matter.

When you stir a whole-grain starter, you will see a world of texture, often spongelike, underneath the surface. When you stir a white starter, you may hear the sound of popping bubbles. These are typical characteristics.

How to Make a Starter

Making a sourdough starter is where the fun begins; it literally feels like magic as it comes alive. In reality, the activity is the result of the natural wild yeast in the flour responding as you mix it with water and allow it time to ferment. The process is simple and only requires very little actual input, just one quick action per day, and then it is all down to giving the starter time and letting it happen.

Even if you already have a working starter, you may find it useful to revisit how to make one to be able to strengthen yours, or a new one as a reminder, or one with some new flour to see how different flours produce differently textured and flavored starters.

One key thing to know when making a starter is that they do not work to a timetable. Starters will be ready when they are ready. Some take 5 days, some take 5 weeks; they are all different, and there is no single answer to the questions of "When will it be ready?" The beauty of this process is in letting it happen, not fretting about it, and following the steps.

Always, always keep going. Making a starter will include exciting active days and flat worrying inactive days, and they are all normal and all part of the process. If in doubt, keep going!

Before you begin, these are my recommendations for making your starter:

Flour: You can make a starter with any wheat-based flour, but if this is the first time you have ever made a sourdough starter, I would recommend using strong white bread flour, typically labeled either "bread flour" or "strong white flour," depending on what part of the world you live in. If you choose to use other flours, the directions remain the same. I recommend using fresh flour; older bags of flour can lose their potency over time.

Note:

If you choose to make a new starter using whole wheat or dark rye flour, you may need to increase the initial amount of water by 10 to 20 grams (1 to 2 tbsp) if the mixture seems very dry.

Water: I use tap water in my starter, but not all tap water is suitable for making sourdough. Consequently, I would always advise using filtered water if you are unsure. If your water is heavily chlorinated, fill a jug with water and leave it on the counter for 24 hours for the chlorine to evaporate. Later, you can test your tap water in a small portion of your starter to see whether it can be used. If your starter does not respond as it usually would, it will show that the tap water is not good enough quality.

Water can be at room temperature or cool.

I do not recommend using distilled, purified or reverse osmosis water for your starter.

Scale: A digital scale makes a huge difference when making a starter. Being able to weigh equal amounts of flour and water really helps not only to create the starter, but also when it comes to maintaining it and making bread dough. I have included cup measurements for readers who would rather use them; they do not translate exactly to the weights that I prefer to use, but they will still work fine.

Container: I like to use a glass bowl or squat glass jar with a fitted lid for keeping a starter. I recommend glass because it does not hold bacteria, smells or flavors from previous foods, but also because it enables you to see the growth of your starter. And I recommend bowls or squat jars rather than tall jars because it is easier to work with a starter in a wider opening than the smaller opening on a taller jar. Ceramic is a good alternative option if you do not have glass.

My preference is to use round rather than square containers that hold around 600 milliliters (2½ cups).

Time: As noted, starters take as long as they need to be ready to use. Each will let you know when it is ready; I have provided details of what to look for in my guide.

Temperature: As with every element of making sourdough, room temperature makes a big difference. Cold temperatures slow your starter down, and warm or hot temperatures speed your starter up. Heat can spoil starters and doughs. Hence, notes about room temperature are included throughout this book.

For making a starter, 68°F (20°C) is the ideal temperature. If your kitchen is much warmer or colder, see "Making a Starter in Hot or Cold Temperatures" (page 16).

Removal: When instructed to remove half of the starter, take out half by eye and place it in another covered bowl. Each time you are instructed to do this, it is important to do so, otherwise you will end up with much more starter than you need, which can make your starter sluggish and weak. Save all of the starter you remove as you go along; you will be able to use it in other recipes. The removed starter is called *discard* and at this point is still weak, so it is best used in recipes where it provides only flavor but does not lift.

Actions: The instructions require one short action per day; this can be done at a time that suits you, around every 24 hours. It does not need to be at exactly the same time every day. You do not need to set a timer—starters cannot tell time. And if you happen to miss a day for any reason, all is not lost—carry on from where you left off; your starter will be fine.

Utensils: Always stir your starter with a clean, stainless-steel fork or spoon. And always clean it immediately after use; otherwise, the starter will dry on it like concrete. If that does happen, soak the utensil in cold water for at least 10 minutes, until the starter softens and can be washed away.

The lid: When the directions state to add a "loose lid," the lid needs to have a very slight opening to allow gases to escape. If you are using a glass container with a lid and a seal, such as a preserving jar, remove the seal and that will be sufficient; or if your container has a plastic lid, lift one small part of it to create an opening.

Starter Guide Step by Step

Here is what to do day by day to create your starter:

Day 1: In a glass or ceramic bowl, mix 50 grams (½ cup) of strong white bread flour, or a different flour of your choice, with 50 grams (¼ cup) of water. Remember that if you are using a whole-grain flour, add an extra 10 to 20 grams (1 to 2 tbsp) of water if the initial mixture is too stiff to stir.

Stir the mixture well, scrape down the sides of the bowl and mix it all in; it will be nicely thick, like porridge, or slightly stiffer if you are using a whole-grain flour. Loosely cover the bowl, allowing a slight opening in the lid if it has one, or cover the bowl with a plate or beeswax wrap, leaving a very slight opening. Leave the bowl on the kitchen counter.

Day 2: Bubbles may already be starting to appear on the surface of your mixture; it may also be very glutinous and bouncy after you finish this first feeding. If not, that is normal, too.

Add 30 grams (¼ cup) of your flour and 30 grams (⅛ cup) of water, stir it well, scraping down the sides of the bowl again and mix it all in, then loosely cover the bowl again and leave it on the counter.

Day 3: Bubbles should be appearing now and it may be starting to smell interesting. An eggy or cheesy odor is not unusual at this point. Add 30 grams (¼ cup) of your flour and 30 grams (⅛ cup) of water, stir it well, scraping down the sides of the bowl and mix it all in, then loosely cover the bowl and leave on the counter.

How to Create a Starter

Follow the steps for making your starter, preferably using a scale to weigh the flour and water for each action.

Stir well each time, using a clean spoon, until the mixture is thick and well mixed.

Scrape around the container, replace the lid loosely and leave it on the counter until the next day, then complete the next step.

This photo is a perfect example of an active starter, ready to use.

Around this time, new starters typically begin to look bubbly, and it is really exciting to see; this is the bacteria and yeast doing their work. However, do not be fooled into thinking that your starter is ready to use. It is not strong enough yet; these changes are all part of the life cycle of making a starter. The bubbles will typically subside over the next few days, but then they will return and stay for longer.

Day 4: Your starter may now be smelling vinegary; that is normal—it indicates the fermenting process is happening. Remove half of the contents of the bowl—you can do this by eye; it does not need to be an exact measurement. Place the sourdough discard in a bowl in the fridge and save it to make recipes such as pancakes and crackers.

Add 30 grams (¼ cup) of your flour and 30 grams (⅛ cup) of water, stir well, scrape down the sides of the bowl, then loosely cover the bowl and leave on the counter.

Day 5: If your starter is now looking less active and bubbly, do not be disheartened; it is all part of the process. Stick with it and keep building the strength in your starter. Add 30 grams (¼ cup) of your flour and 30 grams (⅛ cup) of water, stir well, scrape down the sides of the bowl, then loosely cover the bowl and leave it on the counter.

Day 6: Remove half of the contents of the bowl. Again, literally take out half and add this to the other discarded starter you have kept in the fridge. Add 30 grams (¼ cup) of your flour and 30 grams (⅛ cup) of water, stir it well, scraping down the sides of the bowl again and mixing it all in, then loosely cover the bowl and leave it on the counter again.

Day 7: Hopefully, you are now seeing bubbles all the way through the mixture. White flour starters can look really exciting now—bubbly and even volcanic. Add 30 grams (¼ cup) of your flour and 30 grams (⅛ cup) of water, stir well, scraping down the sides of the bowl, then loosely cover the bowl and leave it on the counter.

Is My Starter Ready to Use?

By now, your starter could be ready to use. If it is a white flour starter, the consistency should be thick and glutinous; if it is whole wheat or whole grain, it should be wonderfully textured and nicely thick.

After the starter has been fed and has had time to grow and blossom to double its size (thus becoming fully "active"), the bubbles should be all the way through the liquid. If you are not sure, repeat the same process again from day 4 onward, alternately feeding, and discarding and feeding, every other day, until your starter is routinely becoming active and doubling in size within several hours after feeds. This may take 2 more days, it may take 2 more weeks, but always keep going.

Starters also get stronger in power and flavor the older they get. The more you use them, the better they will get.

Once your starter is established, keep the lid firmly shut tight and store it in the fridge until you are ready to use it in a recipe. This puts your starter to sleep while you do not need it. From this point on, you no longer need to keep discarding and feeding; when you are going to use it, feed it as explained in the following sections.

Always aim to keep a base amount of only 100 grams (½ cup) or less of starter at any time. This is a perfect base amount to keep your starter lean, healthy and active. If you have built up more than that, use some up in some recipes to reduce how much you store.

Making a Starter in Hot or Cold Temperatures

In hot temperatures, when the room temperature is over 77°F (25°C), store your starter in the fridge during the hottest parts of the day to prevent it from becoming thin and weak. If that does happen, add extra flour to your starter to thicken it back up to its previous thickness. If it becomes thin again, add extra flour again. You can do this as often as you need to keep it glutinous and healthy. The reason it may become thin and weak is that warmth increases the yeast activity in the starter, so it eats up the food in the flour faster than at cooler temperatures. Adding more flour at feeding times will keep your starter full and happy.

In cold temperatures, when the room temperature is under 64°F (18°C), it can be hard to get a new starter active and responsive. In this situation, use finger-warm water, about 100°F (38°C)—but not hotter than that—to feed your starter, and find a warm place for it to sit and respond to its feed. Try using your oven with just the pilot light on, or set it by a heater or a warm radiator. Some people also like to put it in their microwave or oven with a bowl of boiled or hot water to create that warm, cozy environment. Do not let it get too warm for too long, though; use the heat source for just long enough for it to grow and bubble, then move it away to a cooler spot until the next feed.

Things to Look Out For

If your starter becomes a thin liquid at any time, feed it flour only and thicken it up, then manage the thickness as you continue making it. It is responding to either its environment or the flour you are using.

If at any time your starter develops a murky gray liquid across the top, do not worry; it is not ruined. It is just letting you know that it is hungry and needs feeding.

If this does happen, you have two options: You can either stir in the liquid and feed it as usual, or pour it away and feed it as usual. This liquid is often called "hooch" as it is alcohol produced by overfermentation of the starter mixture; by stirring it in, you help build the flavor of your starter. This does not mean, however, that your starter is now alcoholic. If you are concerned, pour the liquid away and ensure that it does not occur again by keeping a careful eye on your starter and your room temperature. Starters produce this liquid either as a result of not being used, and therefore fed, for a period of time, or because they have become warm, which makes them work faster and overferment.

If your starter develops a hard, dry top layer, it is getting too dry on the top, which will also prevent it from growing. This can happen if you live in a dry environment. Scrape off the dry layer, feed as usual and keep your starter firmly covered to protect it from now on.

If your starter develops pink or orange spots or your jar develops white, black or green furry bits, this is mold; sadly, your starter cannot be saved from this. It should be totally discarded and the container fully cleaned to reuse; you will need to start again.

Start with your base amount of 100 g (½ cup) or less of starter; using a scale, add the amount of flour you wish to feed it.

Add an equal weight of water (the same weight as the flour).

Using a clean spoon or fork, stir it well, scraping down the sides and stirring everything together.

The mixture does not need to be stirred until completely smooth; lumpy is okay. Then firmly replace the lid, leave it on the counter and allow it to respond and become ready to use.

If your starter resembles a gluey or smooth, untextured consistency and shows no sign of change whatever you do, this is due to the flour you are using. The flour may be too weak or old for the job. In this instance, I would recommend removing three-quarters of the starter and feeding the remainder with a new flour. If there continues to be no response, I would recommend starting afresh with the new flour.

How to Use Your Starter in Recipes

When you want to make your dough, remove your base starter from the fridge and feed it with the amount of flour and water necessary to generate the amount of starter you will need for the recipe.

For example, if the recipe calls for 50 grams (¼ cup) of starter, I feed my base amount of starter with 30 grams (¼ cup) of flour and 30 grams (⅛ cup) of water. This way, I will have enough to remove for the recipe and will still have the same amount of the base that I started with, plus an extra 10 grams or so, which is often lost to the spoon or mixing utensils anyway. To generate more starter, feed it more flour and water and allow it sufficient time to respond to the bigger feed.

Stir your starter well until no dry flour is visible; it should have a thick batterlike consistency. You do not need to stir it endlessly, though; it does not need to be perfectly mixed—lumpy is fine.

Scrape down the sides of your bowl or jar, and mix any dried flour or starter into the starter. Keeping your bowl or jar tidy helps keep your starter healthy.

Replace the lid firmly and leave it to respond and become active.

Top Tip:

You do not need a bigger base amount of starter to be able to produce a larger amount for a recipe. The base amount never needs to change, just how much flour and water you feed it.

Maintaining Your Starter Efficiently and Effectively

This is a scenario when less is truly more. Storing a small amount of starter as your base amount keeps it active and healthy; if you fall into the trap of keeping large jars of starter, it will become weak and sluggish and will take a lot of flour to maintain it. Keep it lean, and keep it keen!

This is my guide for maintaining a lean, active, healthy starter:

- Only ever keep 100 grams (½ cup) or less of starter at any time. This is a perfect base amount.

- Always feed all of your starter, not a portion or part of it. This way, your starter gets a workout with every feed, which builds its strength with every use.

- Only ever feed your starter based on what you will need for the recipe you are making; this way, you will never produce any waste.

How to Convert Your Starter to New Flours

Feed your starter 30 grams (¼ cup) of flour plus 30 grams (⅛ cup) of water and allow it to become active. Once it has responded and grown, remove 50 grams (¼ cup) of your starter, place it into a fresh, clean glass bowl with a lid or in a glass jar and start feeding it with your chosen flour. The more you use it and feed it with the new flour, it will become completely converted. Of course, you could also simply use the same process to make a new starter with a new flour.

Understanding YOUR Starter

The key to working successfully with sourdough is to understand your starter. As in all things sourdough, it becomes very easy to compare your starter with others, to look at photos or videos online and worry that yours does not look the same. But the fact is, unless your starter is made from exactly the same flour and water and lives in the same kitchen, it will never be the same. And it does not need to be.

All your starter needs to do is work. When you feed it, it needs to respond by growing in size, and it needs to lift your dough and your loaves. As long as it does that, it is working and is successful.

I highly recommend keeping notes about how your starter behaves (see "How to Keep a Sourdough Journal" [page 186]). This way, you will be able to see the pattern in your starter's behavior, which will help you to plan your bakes. The more you use your starter and make these notes, the more you will know what you are looking for and the more relaxed you will be about using it.

Each time you want to use your starter, make a note of what time you feed it, whether you feed it at cold or room temperature, what the temperature is in your kitchen when you feed it, whether you use cold or warm water, what flour you use and where in your kitchen you then place it. Then, note what time when it has doubled in size and become active.

If you would like to truly understand it, take a leap of faith and allow your starter to start to drop and become less active again and note how long it takes to happen. All the way through, make a note of the look, smell and consistency.

By doing this throughout the year, you will also create a picture of how the different seasons and temperatures affect your starter and how they need to be taken into account when planning to make dough.

As an example, when I feed my starter, I feed it at room temperature with cold or cool water. It takes my starter an average of 4 hours to become active and to have grown and flourished. I know that in the summer it will take a bit less time, and in the winter it may take an hour or so longer. I know this from watching and noting the activity of my starter.

Managing Your Starter for Your Home and Life

By observing and documenting the behavior of your starter, you will see a pattern and you will be able to apply that to your dough making as well as fitting it in with life. Here are a few tips on this topic:

- If your kitchen is cold and you would like to speed up your starter's response to its feed, use warm water when you feed it and keep it in a warm spot in your kitchen, just not too warm or for too long.

- If your kitchen is warm, feed your starter as normal, and keep a close eye on it. This is not the time to set it aside somewhere and forget about it for a few hours. Do not let it become hungry or thin. A thin starter is a weak starter, and it will not be strong enough to rise the dough.

- If your kitchen is warm and your starter is growing too quickly for your dough plans, if it has become very bubbly or it has nearly doubled in size and you are not ready to use it, put it back in the fridge to slow it down. When you are ready to use it, either use it directly from the fridge, or allow it to warm up briefly at room temperature.

- If you fed your starter in readiness to use it, but life has other ideas and you cannot use it as planned, put it in the fridge. When you are ready to use it, take it from the fridge, allow it to warm up and finish its feed, then use when ready.

- If the flour in your starter is whole grain and you feel your starter is thick and not growing, add extra water to loosen it up. Give it small amounts of water at a time, 5 to 10 grams (1½ tsp to 1 tbsp) only, and feel your way to a batter-like consistency.

- If at any time your starter becomes thin, it is becoming weak. It will probably smell strongly too because it is hungry. Feed it flour only to thicken it back up to its previous consistency. Allow it time to respond, then feed it as usual going forward. Assess why it became thin (Was it too warm? Is your flour soft and weak?) and ensure that it does not keep happening. If it does, it is okay to give it whatever flour it needs at any time to manage its consistency and strength.

To be able to assist you in using your starter efficiently and in varying ways, I have tested my starter, using it at different times and different points of its life cycle. Consequently, I can reassure you that if you are not there exactly at the point that your starter reaches its growth peak, or if you are not really sure what the peak looks like, all is not lost.

The *peak* is the highest point that your starter grows to after feeding. It will grow and blossom and hit a peak, which it will stay at for a period of time before it then slowly starts to drop back down again. But this does not mean that it is no longer useable for your dough. Having been fed, your starter can now be used at any time after growing, peaking and dropping, as long as it does not become thin at any time. A thin starter is a weak starter and will need to be fed again before use.

As long as your starter retains its glutinous, batter-like consistency after being fed, it can be used without being fed again.

How to Boost Your Starter

If your starter has become inactive or weak, it may benefit from a boost. A weak starter tends to be flat and sluggish, or thin with tiny bubbles on the surface, and struggles to make a dough grow and proof.

Try a flour boost: Feed your starter from a new bag of flour. Old flour can lead to starters becoming inactive. This can be a fresh bag of the same make and type of flour, or a different type of flour. Sometimes a change is as good as a rest, and the infusion of new flour is enough to boost a slow starter.

If you do not want to risk your entire starter by feeding it with a different flour, split your base amount of starter in two; continue to feed one half with the same flour as previously used. Feed the other half with a different flour. For example, whole wheat, whole-grain spelt or whole-grain einkorn flour may boost a white flour starter, or vice versa.

Alternatively, follow a feeding boost: Twice a day (once in the morning and once in the evening), for 2 days (48 hours), remove half of your starter, then feed it 30 grams (¼ cup) of your chosen flour plus 30 grams (⅛ cup) of water and store it at room temperature, firmly covered, for a total of four feedings. Your starter should show more activity after this time. Continue to store and use it as usual from this point.

Do Not Always Assume Your Starter Is to Blame

If your loaf has not grown and baked as you hoped it would, sourdough bakers often assume this is the fault of the starter; it is a very easy assumption to make, but it is rarely actually the issue.

There are many reasons that a dough may not have produced the loaf you expected, but there is a key marker about whether the issue is your starter:

- If your dough grows during the main bulk proof, your starter is working perfectly. The growth of the dough shows you that.

- If your dough is slow to grow, take into account the overnight temperatures; if it was cold overnight, dough will take longer to fully grow. If you included whole-grain flours or extra ingredients in your dough, the dough will take longer to fully proof. Allow it more time to complete its proof.

- If the temperature overnight remained between 64 and 68°F (18 and 20°C) and your dough was slow to grow, then your starter may be weak and needs a boost.

- If the temperature overnight remained between 64 and 68°F (18 and 20°C) and your dough did not grow at all, *then* the issue is very likely to be your starter. In this case, give it a boost.

The final word is: Starters are very resilient. They are rarely dead. They may be slow or weak, but they are very rarely dead and can always be nurtured back to health. Do not ever give up on them or throw them away, unless there is mold.

Timetables for Feeding and Using Your Starter

Over the past couple of years, I have spent a lot of time experimenting with using my starter, pushing it to see just how simple I can make this process for myself and, therefore, for you. I am very happy to say that I can now share with you that there is a lot more freedom in using a starter than you may have originally thought; I have always focused on the simplicity of the process of making sourdough, and being able to share new ideas and ways of using a starter brings even more simplicity to everything I do. Never again do you need to be held hostage by your starter or your dough; this can truly be a simple and stress-free process.

The best way to use your starter is the way that works best for YOUR starter and YOUR home. In this section, you will find some schedules for feeding and using your starter, which you can tie in with the schedules for preparing your doughs (pages 61–63).

I highly recommend trying each of the schedules at different times to see which works best for you. You may find that there is one that you like and your starter responds well to, or one that you tweak for yourself.

As with everything, as I always say, there is no right or wrong here; all that matters is personal preference and whatever works for you.

My preferred way of using my starter is to take it from the fridge, let it come up to room temperature, feed it flour and water, then leave it to become bubbly and active. That is when I like to use it. But I also know, and can share with you, that there are other ways and times that you can use your starter. These schedules will give you some other ideas but will also include signs for you to look for, to know when your starter really cannot be used. Hopefully, these tips and guidelines will give you some ideas for using your starter in different ways to fit in with you and your life. Sometimes the standard straightforward timetable does not work for you, or life gets in the way, so knowing that you have options gives you a lot more flexibility in your sourdough making.

My Standard "Feed It to Use It" Schedule

9:00 a.m.: Take your starter from the fridge and place it on the counter to warm up, keeping the lid firmly on.

11:00 a.m.: Feed your starter per your dough requirements, replace the lid and leave on the counter to respond.

4:00 to 6:00 p.m.: Assuming your starter has responded to the feed and has grown and become active, remove what you need to make your dough, then return the rest of the starter to the fridge until next time.

The "Night Before" Schedule

This is useful if you want to be able to make dough first thing in the morning.

In the evening: Feed your starter directly from the fridge and replace the lid. Leave the starter on the counter all night.

In the morning: Use your starter to make your dough without feeding it again. Return the rest of the starter to the fridge until next time.

Note:

The only time this will not work is if it is very warm overnight and your starter becomes thin and inactive as a result.

The "Use It First, Then Feed It After" Schedule

This is useful if you want to be able to make dough without the forward planning and time necessary to feed and activate your starter. If you are keeping a base amount of 100 grams (½ cup) of starter, as I do, and have fed your starter within the last 2 weeks, this can work for you.

Take your starter from the fridge and remove what you need for your recipe, assuming it is less than 100 grams (½ cup). Then, feed the remaining starter to replenish the base amount.

Put the lid back on your starter, allow it to become active, then place it back in the fridge. Next time, you can use it directly without feeding it again, then follow the same process again.

Note:

The only times this will not work is if your starter has become thin and inactive since it was last fed.

The "Fed It but Had to Go Out" Scenario

If you fed your starter in readiness to use it, but suddenly your plans have changed, put it back into the fridge. Get it out again when you are ready to make your dough. The fridge suspends your starter in that moment; often, it even looks the same when you take it out again as when you placed it in the fridge.

Assuming this is within 2 weeks of feeding it, use it directly without needing to feed it again.

Note:

The only times this will not work is if your starter has become thin and inactive since it was last fed.

Feeding the Scraps

If you find that you have somehow managed to use all of your starter, and you have been left with just scrapings in your bowl or jar, do not despair. And do not clean out the bowl, whatever you do!

Amazingly, there is enough power still in that bowl to rebuild a starter.

Add 50 grams (½ cup) of the flour of your choice and 50 grams (¼ cup) of water to the bowl, stir it well, place the lid firmly on the bowl and leave it on the counter. In 24 to 36 hours, you should be rewarded with an active, replenished starter.

Feed it again to build the quantity back up or to use it.

How to Dry Starter for Long-Term Storage

Drying out some of your starter is a great way to produce some backup starter for your own reassurance and also a great way to share your starter with others. Drying out starter is a really easy process, and it means that you will always have a fallback. See step-by-step photos on the next page.

You will need:

- Your starter
- Good-quality parchment paper or a silicone baking sheet
- A clean stainless-steel tablespoon
- Fine-mesh food cover

Feed your starter and allow it to grow and respond.

I would recommend feeding your starter two or three times your usual feeding amount to produce more active starter on this occasion and maximize this drying opportunity.

Once active, lay a large sheet of good-quality parchment paper or a silicone baking sheet on an area of your kitchen counter where it can remain for 2 to 3 days. Do not use waxed paper or a paper towel; the starter will stick and will not come off once dried.

Spoon the active starter onto the sheet, leaving your standard base amount in the bowl or jar, then use the back of the spoon to spread the starter as thinly as possible on the paper. The thinner it is, the faster it will dry out. Try as much as possible to avoid creating thick spots; any globs of starter will take a very long time to dry completely.

Cover the paper with the mesh food cover and leave for 2 to 3 days, or until fully dried out. I always air dry mine; if you have a dehydrator, you can make it go faster.

Once dried, it will be a darker color and will start to lift off the sheet itself. Fold the sheet to break up the dried starter (this way, you do not need to actually handle it). Make sure the starter is completely dried to prevent it from developing any mold in storage. If the starter bends in any places instead of breaks, it needs to keep drying—return the sheet to your counter to dry until your starter is fully ready to store. Tip the broken bits of dried starter into a clean jar. You can leave it in larger pieces or break it down more in a clean blender.

Now, test your dried starter to ensure that it will revive successfully.

(continued)

How to Dry Out Starter

Feed your starter. Once active, spoon the amount you want to dry out onto a sheet of parchment paper.

Use the back of your spoon, or a spatula, to spread the starter as thinly as possible over the paper.

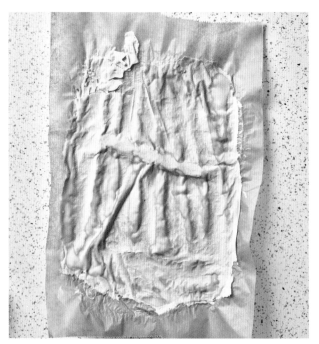

Cover it with a fine mesh food cover and leave it to air dry until completely dried and hard. This may take 24 hours or more.

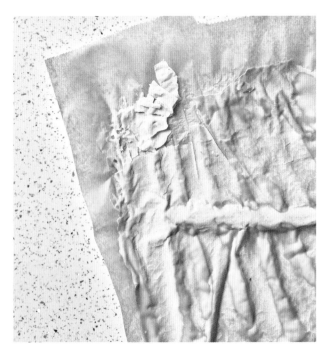

Once the starter is fully dried and easily lifts off the paper, remove it all, break it up into pieces and store it in a clean jar.

To revive dried starter, in a bowl, mix 20 grams (⅛ cup) of the dried starter pieces with 80 grams (¾ cup) of flour and 90 grams (¼ cup plus 2 tbsp) of water. It will be a thick mixture; the dried starter will not dissolve; you will be able to see it still in the mixture. Stir it well, firmly cover the bowl and leave it for 24 to 36 hours to bubble up and fully come back to life, stirring a couple of times during that time. Once it is fully revived, use it in the usual way.

You can now gift and send portions of the dried starter to friends and family so that they can share your sourdough joy, or you can store it in an airtight container in a cool, dark place for several months or even years. I have successfully revived dried starter after several years.

Top Tip:

Once you have a stock of dried starter, if your starter ever starts to behave differently and has become weak or inactive, add 15 grams (1 tbsp) of your dried starter to your starter. Stir well, cover and leave it for 24 to 36 hours to respond. It will boost your starter with its own saved power.

Troubleshooting Starters & FAQ

Sourdough starters can cause fear and consternation; because our starters are the crux of everything we make, for many bakers, there is a constant concern about their starter's well-being.

The following are some of the typical questions I am asked that I hope will provide some reassurance for you and your starter.

Store the fully dried and broken up starter in a clean, dry jar, and store in a cool, dark place.

When will my starter be ready?

There is no single answer to this; each starter is different and will be ready when it is ready. The most important thing is to let it happen; it will be worth the wait.

How long after feeding can I use my starter?

Again, there is no single answer to this question because it depends on how your starter behaves plus room temperature. If it is cold, your starter will take longer to become active after feeding than if it is warm.

Why does my starter not look like yours?

It does not need to. They all look different—the flour you use, the water and your environment all make a difference to how your starter will look; focus on how it works, not how it looks.

Why is my starter not bubbly?

It will depend on the flour it is made from; not all flours produce a bubbly starter, but this does not mean it is not a strong starter. Look for growth instead.

Can I use my starter from cold?

Yes, you can, it may just take your dough a little longer to rise as the starter warms up.

I have not fed my starter for a few days; can I use it without feeding it?

Yes, you can. As long as your starter has been stored happily in the fridge, fed within the last 2 weeks and has not become thin, you can use it without feeding it.

Do I need to let my starter come up to room temperature before feeding it?

No, you can feed it from cold if you like; it will just take a little longer to respond as it wakes up. You can help it along by using finger-warm water, about 100°F (38°C), to feed it.

Why is my starter thin with small bubbles?

This will happen if your starter has become weak from being too warm. The heat will make your starter work quickly and eat through its flour, making it thin and producing tiny bubbles on the surface. In this situation, feed it extra flour to thicken it up and give it some strength back. Also consider where you have been keeping your starter and what made it become thin in the first place, and consider moving it somewhere else. A thin starter tends to be a weak starter. It can also happen if your flour is weak or old; try a new or stronger bag of flour.

How much starter should I keep?

I always keep a standard base amount of 100 grams (½ cup) or less of my starter. You do not need to keep any more than that, and in fact in this case, less is more. This takes a leap of faith, but you do not need to keep huge jars of starter; apart from anything else, you will be forever maintaining it and feeding it and wasting flour. By keeping less, you keep your starter lean and healthy and fighting fit.

If I need more starter for a recipe, do I need more starter to begin with?

You do not need a bigger base amount of starter to generate more for a recipe; the base amount stays the same. Just feed it extra flour and water to generate more starter for the recipe.

When I feed my starter, do I need to feed it using equal amounts of starter, flour and water?

No, you do not. You do not need to use ratios or equal quantities. Keep a standard base amount and feed your starter based on what you will need for your recipe. For example, to make a single standard dough, I feed my starter 30 grams (¼ cup) flour plus 30 grams (⅛ cup) water. To make two doughs, I double this. For three doughs, I triple it, and so on. But all the time, the base amount remains the same. Note that if you feed your starter two or three times the usual amount, it may take longer to grow and respond.

Do I have to remove or discard starter? I hate wasting flour.

No, you never need to remove any or have any waste when maintaining your starter. When making a new starter, you do need to remove some, but you can store it in the fridge and use it in a recipe; it does not need to be wasted. Plus, if you only feed your starter to use it, and feed it based on how much you will need for your dough, you will never have any waste.

Is my starter dead?

Unless they get moldy, starters are very rarely dead; they are very resilient. It may need a boost (see page 20) or a couple of feeds if you feel it is lackluster, but that is all. Whatever you do, don't throw it away unless it has pink, orange, green or black mold on it.

Is it possible to overfeed a starter?

No, but keep in mind that if you give your starter a bigger feed than usual, it may take longer than usual to become active, as it has more to digest.

As your methods mean that I do not need to produce any discard, how do I produce extra starter for discard recipes?

You can feed your starter to produce whatever you need for any recipe you would like to make. There is no need to keep extra starter or jars of discard for this purpose. Feed it for only what you need.

My starter works really well but it smells awful. Can I fix that?

All starters smell different, but if yours smells really unpleasant, try a different flour. Flour and environment make the difference to how your starter smells; we can control the choice of flour even if we cannot control our environment. A different brand or type of flour may make quite a difference to the smell, and may even enhance the strength. Rather than risk your whole starter to a new flour, separate out a portion, place it in a new bowl or jar and feed it as usual just with a new flour.

How often do I need to change my starter container?

Never. Unless your starter or container has become moldy and therefore needs replacing, there is never any need to change the container that your starter lives in.

If your container has become crusty, use a spoon to scrape off the dried starter and mix it into your starter; it is just dried starter, and will add strength to your starter mixture. If you would like to move your starter, spoon it into a clean container, then soak your crusty container in cold water to loosen the dried starter to be able to clean it. Always aim to scrape down your starter container after every use to keep it tidy and manageable.

INGREDIENTS AND EQUIPMENT

There are certain items that are ideal for making sourdough and that will aid your success with my recipes, especially if you are new to making it. The following is a list of the ingredients and equipment that I use regularly and recommend for any new or existing sourdough baker.

Then, there are other items that are not necessities but nice to have, which I have included in the second half of the list. This includes some other pans that are used in some of my recipes in this book.

There is no pressure to purchase this whole list. I highly recommend seeing what you have in your cupboards that can be used as alternatives.

The Key Items

Flour: You may think that flour is just flour, but I am here to tell you that the flour that you use to make sourdough will make a difference to the outcome of your loaves. It was not until I started making sourdough that I discovered a whole new unknown world of flour. I had purchased and used flour before, but I had bought whatever the recipe told me I needed; I had never thought to question what made them different or why I needed to use a specific type of flour. It was only when I started making sourdough that I became aware of flour and the differences it can make to the outcome of a bake. The strength of a flour, the type of flour, how a flour absorbs water and the history of a flour can all affect how dough develops and how a loaf then bakes in the oven.

Strong white bread flour is a perfect starting point for making sourdough and is the basis of many of the recipes in this book. Look for a flour with 12 to 13 percent protein; this enables you to be able to really stretch the dough when performing the pulls and folds without it breaking, and it gives the dough a strong ideal structure that is needed during the long proofing time that sourdough requires.

Other flours are mentioned throughout the book, and I highly recommend trying them if you have access to them; if not, alternatives are included in the recipe.

Top Tip:

If you are new to making sourdough, I highly recommend choosing a good-quality strong white bread flour and using only that one brand while you learn.

Water: This is a key element in making sourdough. The choice of water used in the dough does make a difference. I use tap water, but if your tap water is not good quality, or heavily chlorinated, I would recommend using filtered water. If your water is heavily chlorinated, you could fill a jug with water and leave it on the counter for 24 hours for the chlorine to evaporate before using it in your dough.

Another aspect that can make a difference is whether your water is hard or soft. Soft water can lead to soft dough that doesn't hold its shape when you try to bake the loaf. If your water is soft, use 30 grams (⅛ cup) less than the recipe states.

Water can be at room temperature or cool.

Salt: Any type of granulated salt can be used in all of the recipes in this book. I prefer Himalayan pink salt, but this is a personal choice rather than affecting the dough or flavor. The same weight of sea salt can be used with no effect on flavor or dough behavior.

I use less salt than most bakers to suit my personal taste; increase it as necessary if you prefer to use more.

Be aware that using iodized salt can leave a bitter aftertaste.

Scale: Using a scale to weigh ingredients is, in my view, a key part of sourdough success. I would recommend using a digital scale, especially if you have had any trouble getting the results you want with sourdough. That said, if you do not have a scale or prefer to use volume measurements, I have included cup and spoon measurements in every recipe.

Room thermometer: Being able to monitor the temperature in your kitchen is a vital step toward sourdough success. I highly recommend having a digital thermometer in your kitchen for just this purpose.

Mixing bowl: I use a standard medium-sized mixing bowl. Mine are 9 inches (23 cm) in diameter and 3½ inches (9 cm) deep and hold 9½ cups (2.25 L), and they are a perfect size for making and proofing my standard full-sized dough.

Banneton: A banneton is a proofing basket that gives loaves shape. They are often made from cane, but wood pulp versions are also available and work really well. The main bannetons I use are round, 8¾ inches (22 cm) in diameter and 3¼ inches (8.5 cm) deep, or 11-inch (28-cm)-long oval bannetons.

A new cane banneton should be prepared prior to using it to ensure that your doughs do not stick to it. Do this by removing the liner, if it came with one, and reconstitute it; spray the inside of the banneton all over with water, then sprinkle a good layer of rice flour all over the inside, too. Leave it to dry to form a nonstick coating. It is now ready to use.

After each use, leave your banneton on the counter to fully dry out, then store it ready for next time, uncovered, in your cupboard. You do not need to clean it or brush out the rice flour, unless it becomes moldy, then it needs to be thoroughly cleaned and dried before preparing it for use again.

Alternatively, wood pulp bannetons do not need to be preprepared in any way; just sprinkle them with rice flour, and brush it all over the inside with your fingers before placing the dough in the banneton. After each use, allow it to fully dry out, then store it, uncovered, in your cupboard.

Rice flour: This is the ideal flour for preparing bannetons to ensure that your dough doesn't stick to them and comes out clean. Rice flour is gluten-free and nonporous, so it does not become sticky like wheat-based flour. You can use white or brown rice flour. If you cannot find rice flour, you can grind uncooked rice to make your own, or use ground semolina or polenta.

Pan: I bake my standard loaves in covered pans. This way, the dough naturally produces steam as it bakes, which is captured inside the pan and helps the rise of the loaves. There is no need to add extra steam to the oven when baking in a covered pan. I use lightweight enamel roasters; Granite Ware pans are a perfect alternative. You can also use a cast-iron Dutch oven or a Le Creuset pan, if you prefer, a carbon steel pan or your choice of baking pan.

For round standard-sized loaves, use a 10¼-inch (26-cm)-diameter round pan.

For oval standard-sized loaves, use a 13¾-inch (30-cm)-long oval pan.

Parchment paper: A good-quality baking parchment paper is ideal for lining your pans when baking loaves. Do not use waxed paper, which will stick to your baked loaves.

Bread lame: This is a handle that holds a razor blade for scoring dough prior to baking.

Wire rack: This is a very necessary item for cooling your baked goodies. It allows your bread to cool evenly and prevents a soggy bottom, which can happen if you place a freshly baked loaf directly on a flat surface.

Useful Items That Are Used in This Book

Shower caps: These are ideal for covering the mixing bowl while the dough proofs; they also allow the dough to grow. They can be used over and over again, are very affordable and come in large packs, so one package will last you a long time.

Bowl scraper: These are ideal for the first mixing of the dough as well as for turning dough out of the bowl where needed.

Other pan sizes: This can be an indulgence and not truly a necessity at all, but I often use an 8-inch (20-cm)-diameter enamel pan with a lid for baking my baby master loaves.

Other loaves are baked differently and details are included in the recipes.

- Sandwich loaves: a 2-pound (900-g) loaf pan, 9 x 5 inches (23 x 14 cm)

- Pullman loaves: a loaf pan with an external size of 8½ x 5 x 4½ inches (21.5 x 12.5 x 11.5 cm), with lid

Loaf pan liners: If you are baking one of my sandwich loaf recipes, loaf pan liners, or parchment paper cut to size, are a perfect way to prevent sticking.

Bundt pan: I use these in a couple of the recipes in this book; my pans are 10½ inches (26.7 cm) in diameter and 4½ inches (11.5 cm) deep, and hold 12 cups (2.8 L).

Useful items to have for making sourdough recipes, especially those in this book. Shown are (starting from top left going counterclockwise) bowl scrapers, bread lame, a shower cap, loaf pan with liner and a smaller lidded enamel pan.

My Master Recipe

My master recipe is the basis of all of my sourdough baking. It is my starting point for every recipe creation. It is also my go-to recipe for making my standard household loaves and the starting point I recommend to bakers new to my methods, or to sourdough at all.

It is a perfect recipe for additions, for scaling up or down in size and for using the dough to make anything sourdough based that takes your fancy. In this section, you will discover how I amend my recipe for making it in different shapes, sizes or pans.

The slow nature of sourdough means that the process of making a standard loaf can stretch across 24 hours, and it is definitely worth the wait. However, if you would like to shorten or lengthen that timescale, I have included tips and timetables for you to be able to do this later in the book.

This version of my recipe includes as much additional information as possible to act as a guide as well as a full recipe. In this main version of my recipe, I use strong white bread flour and make it as a round loaf (*boule*) or as an oval loaf (*batard*) by using differently shaped bannetons. In this recipe, I am making a round loaf, but I have included details of both options in recipes in later sections.

You can also use different flours and add-ins in this recipe, and the loaf can be made and baked in different sizes and shapes as you will see in "The Master Recipe Sourdough Collection" chapter (page 71).

I have included times in the recipe to show the process and timings I use to make my own loaves, and these can act as a guide or be used exactly as written. In the following sections, you will find alternative timetables and notes on how to amend the recipe and timings for yourself.

Note:

Many sourdough making recipes include many more steps than my master recipe; I keep my process as streamlined and simple as possible to ensure that it is relevant and user-friendly. It may seem on first reading that there is a lot of input for this one recipe, but I can assure you that each step is included for a reason and makes a difference to the final outcome of the baked loaf, and I have kept it as minimal as possible.

Makes 1 standard loaf

TIMING: The timeline for making this recipe can span 24 hours, but within that time the actual physical input is a total of 30 minutes.

(continued)

My Master Recipe (Continued)

50 g (¼ cup) starter

350 g (1½ cups) water

500 g (4 cups) strong white bread flour

7 g (1 tsp) salt, or to taste

Supplies
Digital scale

Large mixing bowl, ideally able to hold 9½ to 10½ cups (2.25 to 2.5 L)

Bowl scraper, stainless steel spoon or stiff spatula

Clean shower cap or damp tea towel

Banneton or bowl

Rice flour, for dusting

Enamel pan or other baking pan with a lid

Parchment paper

Lame or razor blade

Wire rack

To Begin

(a) 9:00 a.m.: If your starter has been sleeping in the fridge, take it from the fridge and leave it on the counter with its lid firmly on to come up to room temperature. This makes it easier to feed as the consistency is looser than when it is cold. However, if you forgot to take it out beforehand, you can still feed it as needed from cold; it will just be stiffer to mix.

If it has been living on the counter because you use it so regularly, start at point (b).

(b) 11:00 a.m.: Feed your starter as per your recipe requirements; for my master recipe you will need 50 grams (¼ cup) of active starter; to produce that from your base amount of starter, feed it 30 grams (¼ cup) of flour plus 30 grams (⅛ cup) of water. Stir it well so that it is nicely mixed with no dry flour showing, but it can still a bit lumpy; it does not need to be perfectly smoothly mixed. Cover it again and allow it to become active, during which time it will bloom and grow and become bubbly and textured.

Note:

You can use any starter made with any flour for this recipe. The flour in the starter does not need to match the flour in the recipe.

Gather together your active starter, water, flour, salt and scale ready to make your dough.

Once everything has been weighed out and added to your mixing bowl, stir it all together to form a rough dough.

Use the bowl scraper, or spatula, to scrape down the sides of the bowl and ensure that everything is roughly mixed; cover the bowl and leave it on the counter.

5:00 p.m.

Step 1: Into your mixing bowl, weigh out all the ingredients and mix them together. I use a stainless-steel tablespoon or a large bowl scraper for the initial mix. Mix until you have a shaggy, rough dough. If some bits of dry flour are still visible, it will be fine, but try to incorporate as much flour as possible into the liquid.

Cover the bowl with a clean shower cap or your choice of cover and leave the bowl on the counter for 1 hour; this allows the flour to start absorbing some of the water and for the whole mixture to relax, making it easier to work with. The cover prevents the surface from becoming dry.

(continued)

My Master Recipe (Continued)

6:00 to 6:30 p.m.

Step 2: After an hour or so, perform the first set of pulls and folds by literally lifting a small handful of dough from one side of the bowl, stretching it up and across the rest of the dough, right over to the other side of the bowl. Turn the bowl slightly and repeat as many times as is necessary until the dough feels less sticky and comes together into a soft ball. By doing these pulls and folds, you are building up the structure in your dough and developing the gluten in the flour, which gives the dough strength. This is when the dough is at its most sticky. Once it comes into an almost smooth ball, stop. Cover the bowl again and leave it on your counter.

7:00 p.m.

Step 3: Over the next few hours, do three more sets of pulls and folds on the dough. These do not need to be at fixed amounts of time apart, but between 30 and 60 minutes apart is ideal. These sets will take fewer pulls and folds before the dough comes into a ball. Each time it does, stop, cover the dough and allow it time to sit before doing the next set. Four sets of pulls and folds in total is an ideal number and completing them all makes a difference to the final outcome of the loaf. If you do fewer sets, the dough will have less structure, which will show in your loaf.

Perform the final set before going to bed.

After an hour or so (the dough will not look much different yet), it's time to begin the first pulls and folds.

Take a small handful of dough from one edge, lift and stretch it right across the bowl to the other side.

Slightly turn the bowl, take another small handful, lift and stretch it right across the bowl.

Continue to pull and fold the dough until it comes into an almost smooth ball, then cover and leave on the counter.

After another hour or so, the dough will have spread out, but will not be growing yet.

Perform the next set of pulls and folds until the dough comes into a ball; this will take less actions now.

Perform these sets of pulls and folds three more times, each time stopping when the dough comes into a ball.

After each set, cover the bowl again and leave on the counter. After the final set, cover and leave on the counter for the night.

My Master Recipe (Continued)

9:00 to 10:00 p.m.

Step 4: Leave the covered bowl on the counter overnight, typically 8 to 10 hours, at 64 to 68°F (18 to 20°C). This is when the dough will do its main bulk of work, hence this is often called the bulk proof or bulk ferment. This time is crucial to the outcome of your loaf.

The timing and temperature are here to show my ideal proofing scenario. If it is colder than stated, the dough will need longer to fully proof; if it is warmer, the dough will need to be made differently from the start with less starter. These situations are all covered in detail in the dough section that follows.

7:00 a.m.

Step 5: In the morning, the dough will have grown to double, maybe almost triple, in size. The dough should have a firmness to it and an almost smooth, slightly domed surface.

If it has been cold overnight, the dough may need longer to fully proof, in which case allow it more time and shift the remaining timings accordingly.

Prepare a round banneton, 8¾ inches (22 cm) in diameter and 3¼ inches (8.5 cm) deep, or a lined bowl, with rice flour and set aside a large baking pan with a lid, plus parchment paper.

The dough now needs to be pulled together and placed in the banneton; this is how the dough gains its shape and structure to become a loaf. This is another crucial point of the process; if the dough is not given sufficient tension at this point, the dough will not hold its shape when it is turned out of the banneton to bake. It is easy to be nervous about overhandling the dough now, but a good strong dough will bounce back, whatever you do to it, whereas if you do not give it enough tension, it will be loose and will spread later. Be firm without crushing the dough; it should be full of resistance and you would not be able to crush it anyway, but do not try!

Remove the cover from the bowl and, while the dough is still in the bowl, firmly perform a final set of pulls and folds on the dough to pull it into a ball. To do this, take a small handful of dough from one side of the bowl, then pull the dough up and across the whole dough to the other side; turn the bowl slightly and repeat the action around the whole dough. You should only need to go once around the bowl to do this. You should now have a smooth ball of dough that holds its shape as it sits in the bowl.

Lift and place the dough, smooth side down, in the prepared banneton. Sprinkle extra rice flour down the sides and across the top of the dough, cover it with the same shower cap and place it in the fridge for at least 3 hours, maximum 24 hours.

Note:

You may notice moisture on the inside of the shower cap or bowl cover; this is condensation from the warmth that your starter naturally creates while doing its bulk of work and is normal.

The next morning, the dough will have grown to double its size, maybe even slightly more, and will fill your bowl.

To prepare the dough to be placed into the banneton, perform a set of pulls and folds on the dough.

Lift, pull and fold the dough right across the bowl; turn the bowl slightly and repeat.

Ensure that you give the dough some tension. Do not crush it, but also do not be too gentle—"nicely firm" works perfectly.

Once it comes into a smooth ball that holds its shape, stop.

Turn the bowl over and tip the ball of dough into your whole hand.

Then place it smooth side down into your prepared banneton; this photo shows the underside of the ball of dough, which will then be flipped over and set down into the banneton.

Sprinkle extra rice flour around the sides and over the top of the dough; cover the banneton with the same cover again and place it into the fridge until you are ready to bake.

My Master Recipe (Continued)

10:00 a.m. onward

Step 6: When you are ready to bake, decide whether you would like to bake in a preheated oven or from a cold start. If preheating, set the oven to 425°F (220°C) convection or 450°F (230°C) conventional.

Take your dough from the fridge. Remove the cover from the banneton; place the parchment paper over the top of the banneton and the pan upside down over the top of them both. With one hand under the banneton and one on the pan, turn it all over together to turn the dough out of the banneton and into the pan. Your dough should happily hold its shape and sit proudly in your pan. If it starts to spread slightly, do not be alarmed; all that matters at this point is how it bakes.

Score the dome of dough by using your sharp razor blade or lame, cutting ⅜ inch (1 cm) deep into the dough, from the outside edge inward in a cross meeting in the middle. Scoring the dough encourages it to grow as it bakes and to grow in a way or design of your choosing; unscored dough will still grow but not as much, and may crack and burst at will. Do not be afraid to score the dough; many people fear its deflating as they score it, and it may, but as long as the dough is strong enough, it will bake up beautifully; if not, there is help for you in the following sections.

If you preheated the oven, put the lid on your pan and bake for 50 minutes. If using a cold start, place the covered pan of dough in the oven, set the temperature to 425°F (220°C) convection or 450°F (230°C) conventional, and set a timer for 55 minutes. In both cases, keep the lid on for the full time.

After the baking time for either option, remove the covered pan from the oven. Open the lid to check the loaf. Baking in a lidded pan produces

When you are ready to bake, follow the directions to turn the dough out of the banneton into the pan, score it and bake. See page 66 to see the baked outcome of this dough.

a golden loaf. When you take off the lid, if you feel that your loaf is looking pale, place it back in the hot oven in its pan, minus the lid, for 5 to 10 minutes to brown the loaf to the color of your choice.

Step 7: Once baked, carefully remove the loaf from the pan, saving the parchment paper for next time, and allow the baked loaf to cool on a wire rack for at least an hour before slicing. If you can wait even more than 1 hour it is even better, as sourdough takes a long time to cool, but if you really cannot wait, go for it and enjoy your warm loaf, but keep in mind that if it seems a bit moist or gummy inside, it is because it needed to cool for longer.

For next time: Save the parchment paper that lined your pan to use again. Let your shower cap or bowl cover dry out, then store them to use again. Leave your banneton on the counter to fully dry out, then store it, uncovered, in your cupboard. It does not need to be brushed out or washed.

(continued)

My Master Recipe (Continued)

The Key Points

From my discussions with many bakers over the past few years, and from my own experience, there are two key steps in this recipe that will make the most difference to the outcome.

To Step 4: how the dough proofs. Following is a section all about proofing, why it is necessary, what the main issues can be and the ways to achieve an ideally proofed dough.

To Step 5: pulling the fully proofed dough together to be placed in the banneton. This step ensures that the well-proofed dough gains some shape and tension. If the dough is not given enough tension, it will spread and not hold its shape when it is turned out of the banneton to be baked.

Much as I may be repeating some of what I said within the recipe, it bears repeating. Many bakers are nervous of overhandling the dough, or squashing it, or bursting the bubbles in the dough; do not be. The dough should be pulled together firmly, without being squashed into oblivion. And a well-proofed, structured loaf will not let you squash it into oblivion; it will be full of resistance. So, do not be too timid at that point, and keep in mind that a well-created and -proofed dough will be strong enough to bounce back and grow up again whatever you do to it.

How to Make My Master Recipe as an Oval or Batard

The same recipe and process can be used to create an oval loaf. The only changes are the shape and size of banneton and pan, and how the dough is placed in the banneton.

Prepare an 11-inch (28-cm)-long oval banneton with rice flour and set aside a baking pan, at least 12 inches (30 cm) long with a lid, plus parchment paper.

Follow all the steps up to Step 5. Then, to shape the dough to fit into an oval banneton, lift and pull the dough over itself along one side of the bowl. Turn the bowl around completely to the other side and pull the dough on that side again in a line to create a fat sausage of dough. Place the dough, smooth side down, in the banneton, sprinkling extra rice flour down the sides and across the top of the dough, cover it again with the same shower cap and place it in the fridge for at least 3 hours, maximum 24 hours.

To bake, follow the same guidelines as described in the main recipe.

See step-by-step images on the next page.

To prepare dough for an oval banneton, lift and pull the dough across itself in a line from one side of the bowl to the other.

Turn the bowl right round, 180 degrees, and lift and pull the other side of the dough across itself.

Pull the dough into a thick sausage, almost knitting it together across the top.

To place the dough into the banneton, place your whole hand over the sausage of dough.

Turn the dough out into your hand and then the banneton, smooth side down. Cover and place in the fridge.

When you are ready to bake, have your pan and lame or razor blade ready.

Following the instructions as described, turn the dough out into your lined pan.

Score with one long line, off center, holding the blade at a 45 degree angle.

Bake as per the recipe.

ALL ABOUT DOUGH

Proofing happens when we mix all of the ingredients for our dough, work it by using pulls and folds to build up the structure of the dough, then allow it time to rise and grow and "proof"; this is what gives the dough the power to grow into a risen loaf as it bakes. In the case of sourdough, the pulls and folds that you perform spread the starter throughout the dough; proofing then allows the wild yeast from your starter to ferment, which then makes the dough rise.

Proofing dough can seem like a minefield, especially with sourdough, as there are a couple of anomalies to keep in mind when doing so, but once you grasp those considerations, you will see that it is truly a lot simpler than you may think.

One of the greatest threats to successful proofing that I come across is a fear of spoiling dough; the fear of underproofing leads to overproofing; the fear of overproofing leads to underproofing. It is very easy to overthink making sourdough, and this is one area where that can definitely be the case.

My greatest advice where dough is concerned is to watch your dough and not the clock. This is the best way to truly understand how dough behaves, how it behaves specifically in your kitchen and when it is ready to move on to the next stage. The information in the following pages will help you to know what to look for in your dough.

Understanding How Time and Temperature Affect Proofing

The key difference between making sourdough and standard yeasted breads is time; sourdough takes longer to proof, but it is that extra time that makes it sourdough—it is what develops the texture and flavor of your bread.

It is because of that longer time that the dough can be subject to influences that would not necessarily affect non-sourdough or commercially yeasted doughs in the same way. The extra time needed can worry or confuse bakers, but it is all part of the process; it is actually something to enjoy and embrace, rather than to fear.

And in partnership with time, the success of sourdough making really *is* all about temperature. I cannot stress this point enough, which is why you will see it referred to time again in this section.

As with all living things, sourdough starter and dough responds to heat and cold. In the heat, starters and doughs work a lot faster as the wild yeast ferments more quickly in response to warmth. As a result, they eat through the flour in the mixture and have a tendency to overdo it. On the other hand, in the cold, they respond much more slowly; they digest the food from the flour a lot slower and take a lot more time to do their job.

I often think of my dough as being a living embodiment of myself; when it is very warm, I virtually turn into a human puddle and have no energy left whatsoever, whereas when it is cold, I do not want to move at all; the dough behaves in exactly the same way. Perhaps you may be the same way? So, if it helps you to think about how your dough behaves, think of how we respond to heat and cold. When it is very warm, your dough is susceptible to becoming a sloppy mess; whereas when it is cold, it does not want to do anything! But the good news is that you can control this.

What Is Well-Proofed Dough?

A well-proofed dough is a dough that has grown to its ideal size and has developed the structure and strength to bake into a successful loaf. It may be hard to know how to judge when the dough has reached this point, especially if you are new to sourdough, so, as always, I aim to keep it simple.

A really simple way of judging whether your dough is sufficiently proofed is by using the bowl as your measure. If you can use a bowl that is the same size as mine, 9 inches (23 cm) in diameter and 3½ inches (9 cm) deep, which holds 9½ cups

(2.25 L), you will be able to judge the growth of your dough by whether it fills the bowl. This is based on the standard-size My Master Recipe dough (page 33), using 500 grams (4 cups) of flour.

When I am doing the main bulk proof, whether overnight or during the day, depending on what timetable I am working to, I look for my dough to have a smoothish, slightly upwardly domed surface and to be level with the edges of my bowl. At this point, the dough is a perfectly proofed size. By using a bowl like this as your measure, you will then be able to start to recognize the growth, as well as the look and feel of the dough.

Aim to use a bowl that matches my measurements; it is a bowl that comes to a narrow base. If you use a wide, flat bowl, it will make it harder for the dough to rise or to be able to judge the growth of the dough.

If you do not have a bowl of this exact size or shape, a simple measure is to look for your dough to at least double in size, maybe even a little more than double. To help you to judge that a good tip is to take a photograph of the dough when you have completed the final set of pulls and folds, and then you can use this to compare the dough after its main proof to help you judge the growth.

What Is Underproofed Dough?

Dough that is underproofed will be a lot smaller. It may also be quite stiff, as it has not received the full benefit of proofing well; it may even have some bubbles on the surface where the dough has tried hard to proof and grow, but has not been able to. At this point, the best thing to do is to allow your dough more time.

Underproofing can be a result of a weak starter or, as stated earlier, a cold environment. You will find tips for both of these on pages 19 and 20.

You can still bake your underproofed dough and still produce a loaf; all that will happen is that you will get a different structure and flavor than you would from a more fully proofed dough. This does not mean that you cannot still have a good, tasty loaf from this dough; in fact some people may even prefer it this way. The main difference will be that the loaf is denser with large, uneven holes. As with all sourdough creations, it will still taste great; it would not be any kind of failure, but instead a lesson in how you might like your sourdough to be.

Note:

Some added ingredients can also slow down the growth of dough; for example, garlic or cinnamon. In these cases, allow the dough more time than usual to grow to its fully proofed potential.

You can also tell whether your dough was underproofed by examining the baked result. If your baked loaf did not rise much while baking, has a peak in the middle of the loaf and flat edges, is pale on the outside, has a mix of very large and uneven holes inside the bread, especially toward the top of the loaf, and a denser texture toward the base, these are all signs of underproofing. The loaf will be dense, possibly tough to chew and lacking flavor.

How to Save Underproofed Dough

If your dough has not grown and doubled in size and is therefore underproofed, the solution is as simple as this: give it more time to fully proof. Watch the dough, let it double, then continue with the recipe and use it. If it has been cold, move the dough to a warmer spot, such as sunlight coming through a window, a warmer room, or in the oven with just the pilot light on, to encourage growth, but keep an eye on it. If you leave it anywhere too warm for too long, it will easily move from being underproofed to overproofed.

Underproofed Dough

Underproofed dough will not fill the bowl after its overnight proof; it may have bubbles from trying to proof more.

When you lift and fold the dough it will be firm, possibly sticky.

It will easily come into a ball, as it is not full of life as a well-proofed dough would be.

The dough will come into a smaller ball, not filling the banneton as much as a well-proofed dough.

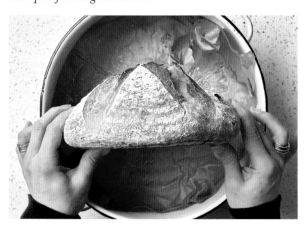

Once baked, the loaf will be smaller, typically with a peak in the middle where it has tried to grow but not been able to.

The inside will have large uneven holes, often toward the top of the loaf, and be denser along the base.

How to Prevent Underproofing

If you know that it is going to be cold when you do the main bulk proof of your dough, follow the tips coming up to give it a starting boost, or allow the dough extra time to fully proof. In the winter, I often proof my doughs for an extra 3 to 4 hours in the morning.

Underproofed doughs are often the result of cold weather, and are therefore frequently the fear of sourdough bakers during winter seasons. In this instance, as I have advised earlier, a little added warmth or an early boost can help the dough, but resist the temptation to leave your dough somewhere warm for the entire night. Many doughs are easily overproofed during the coldest times due to being placed somewhere warm to "help" them proof. For example, an oven with just the pilot light on can be a great help, but only for a few hours at a time; if you leave dough in the oven for the whole night, it will overproof. Likewise, if you have a warm cupboard or proofing drawer, these tools can be very helpful for a short time, but not for long periods.

Top Tip:

Do not use your starter if it is looking flat or thin; you will risk an underproofed dough. Give it a boost (page 20) to strengthen it before using it in a dough.

What Is Overproofed Dough?

Overproofing dough can be a bakers' greatest fear, but it does not need to be. Overproofed dough is still usable, whatever the texture. This section aims to explain overproofing, what to look for, how to prevent it and how to use it if it happens.

If dough is overproofed, that means it has lost its structure and integrity. It will typically still fill the bowl; it may even be trying to escape the bowl after its main bulk proof. It will probably look bubbly and lively and seem very exciting, but as soon as you touch it, it will collapse under your fingertips.

Typical overproofed dough will have a slightly dipped surface that has sunk down with lots of bubbly activity across the top. The dough, when you handle it, will probably be quite sticky and unmanageable. At this point, the dough is not ruined, it just needs to be used differently.

A dough that is hard to shape and score and a resultant baked loaf that is pale, wide and flat, which failed to grow while baking, with a tight crumb of small holes, possibly sticky and shiny, suggests the dough was overproofed. The loaf will be very sour due to the extra proofing.

Overproofed dough tends to be the result of a warm environment and the dough being in that environment for too long. It could also be the result of the dough having been left to bulk proof for too long or being made with too much starter. There are times when some heat and additional starter can be useful for proofing dough, but as with many things, too much of a good thing can prove to be nonbeneficial in this case.

If the culprit was heat, this is because yeast responds to heat; this makes the starter work faster and the dough grows quickly and loses all integrity. It will now not be able to hold its own shape to bake it as a free-form loaf. If you try to, it will be a wide, flat, dense loaf.

Overproofed Dough

Overproofed dough will fill the bowl, possibly even overflow it; it will be bubbly and wobbly.

When you try to pull it together the dough will be sticky and sloppy.

Your hand will likely be covered in sticky, messy dough, and it will be impossible to bring the dough into a firm ball.

The dough will spread in the banneton and will not hold its shape; it will also spread when you turn it out of the banneton to bake and will be difficult to score.

The loaf will typically bake to a wide, flat loaf, filling the base of the pan.

The inside of the loaf will be dense and tight with small holes, and often a damp texture.

How to Recognize Whether a Dough Is Overproofing and How to Save It

One of my most key tips when making sourdough is to learn to watch the dough and not the clock. This is never of more importance than in the case of overproofing dough; the dough will show you what is happening.

A dough that is heading toward overproofing will do so when it is warm; warm dough is soft and stretchy and great to handle in its initial stages, and it will then grow in size quickly. It can literally grow before your eyes, which is the first sign that you may need to slow it down by placing it somewhere cooler. This could be in the fridge until you want to use the dough; it will continue to grow in the fridge as it cools down, then come to a stop. Allow it to come back up to room temperature to make it easier to handle when you want to use it.

As it continues to overproof, dough will get very sticky and will be very wobbly if you move the bowl. It will continue to grow at speed, getting looser and stickier and bubbly, until it mushrooms out of the bowl and down the sides. It will stick to your chosen bowl cover and anything else it touches. At this point, as soon as you touch the dough, if it has not already, it will collapse inward into a sticky mess.

If you have not been awake to see these stages, the first sign that your dough overproofed will be an inwardly dipped, bubbly, sticky dough.

If you now try to handle the dough or bring it into any kind of ball, it will be impossible. At this stage, do not throw it away and waste it; there are a few options for how you can use it. Over-proofed dough is always full of flavor and should not be wasted. These are my recommendations of how to use it:

If it has become very liquid, whisk in enough milk to make a batter and use it to make pancakes. Or mix in some yogurt and make flatbreads.

If it still has some body to it and you can handle the dough, pull it into a loose ball, place it into a lined sandwich loaf pan, or a Pullman loaf pan, and follow the processes from Step 5 onward in My Master Recipe (page 33); allow the dough to proof again and bake per My Master Recipe (page 33) or the recipes in "The Master Recipe Sourdough Collection" chapter (page 71). Or scrape it into a pan and use it to make focaccia per the recipe on page 148, from Step 5 onward.

How to Prevent Overproofing

If you have been proofing the dough during the day and are able to see the dough in action, the point at which to stop the dough from further proofing, and heading toward overproofing, is once the dough has doubled in size. At that point, stop the dough from proofing any further in the bowl and pull it together to go into your banneton and into the fridge. This is how you will save it from overproofing.

If your dough has overproofed, the best way to prevent it from happening again is to note the circumstances that made it happen. The culprit will typically be heat and/or time. If you can review what temperatures may have led to over-proofing, this will help you to head that off it in the future.

If you are concerned about it happening again, there is a simple solution: use less starter. This will slow down the dough growth. Use half of the amount of starter stated in the recipe as a starting point. You can reduce it even more if necessary next time. You do not need to amend any of the other quantities.

The best way to really understand how under-proofed dough occurs, looks, feels and behaves is to experience it for yourself. It is also the best way to take away the fear of overproofing. Once you have experienced it for yourself and realized that it is not as terrible as it sounds and not the end of the sourdough world, it will give you a sense of freedom. Whether you intentionally overproof a batch of dough to experience this, or it just happens to occur to you, I highly recommend seeing this as a positive learning experience.

Note:

Even in cold months, it is possible to overproof dough; central heating, the heat that kitchen appliances produce and residual heat from ovens and cooking can all make your kitchen warmer and for longer than you think. Once again, this is why having a room thermometer is so useful for making sourdough and understanding what can affect it.

Adding Extras to Your Doughs and the Effect That Has

Dough is a wonderful vehicle for adding flavors and ingredients to; there really is no end to the possibilities. That said, which extras you choose to add to your dough can make a difference to how it grows and bakes. Seeds or cheese, for example,

add weight to the dough; the dough therefore may not rise as much as it would without them, and the baked loaf may be denser. But that is typical and the loaf will taste great. There is no need to feel like the baked loaf is not a good one because it's not as risen as a plain dough.

The same goes for whole-grain flours. Making doughs with whole wheat or any whole-grain or ancient grain flours can also lead to heavier, denser loaves, which is again typical and idiosyncratic of breads made with whole-grain flours. These loaves always taste wonderful, but they will not be as light and fluffy as standard white flour loaves, and the two should never be compared.

When adding extra ingredients to a standard full-size dough, such as My Master Recipe (page 33), follow the following maximum amounts as a guide. If you exceed these quantities, you may need to increase the size of your dough or the amount of water in your dough. Add any of these extras to your dough when you first mix it.

- 150 grams (5.5 oz) or less of fully cooked and cooled grains
- 150 grams (5.5 oz) or less of grated or chunks of cheese
- 100 grams (3.5 oz) or less of seeds and nuts
- 100 grams (3.5 oz) or less of dried fruits
- 100 grams (3.5 oz) or less of chocolate chips or chunks

Herbs and spices do not affect the weight of the dough and no amendments need to be made to add them to a dough—for example, no reduction of flour or addition of water is needed.

Sticky Doughs

Sticky dough can worry bakers; it is easy to assume that sticky dough is a problem dough. This section will explain what can make dough sticky and whether it needs to be amended.

When you mix and start working with a new dough, it is always sticky initially, but typically becomes less so with each handling; however, some doughs never lose the stickiness. A sticky dough can be the result of the flour that you have used in the dough: Some bread flours absorb water more than others and therefore create a stickier dough, and some ancient grain or whole-grain flours, such as einkorn or rye flour, produce sticky doughs. And in this case, if you are happy with your baked loaves, go with it and embrace the sticky dough.

If your dough is sticky, try wetting your hands slightly to handle it, *but* do not wet them too much; otherwise, you are adding more water to the dough and may actually increase its stickiness.

If you feel that the dough was too sticky from the start and that your loaves could have a better shape or bake, try using 30 grams (⅛ cup) less water in your dough next time; this should be sufficient to reduce the stickiness and help your dough keep its shape.

If you have ruled out the flour you have used, then a sticky dough might be telling you a story of a proofing issue, either under- or overproofing, which would result in a sticky dough after the main proof. In this case, refer to page 51 for more information and guidance. If your dough is sticking to the proofing bowl, see page 54 in the following troubleshooting section; if it is sticking to the banneton, see page 55.

A Note About Dough

There is nothing to say that there is anything wrong with underproofed or overproofed dough, but I highly recommend working to a point of fully proofed dough so that you can judge for yourself how you prefer your bread. Some people like less-proofed dough because it has a less sour taste and they like a denser loaf; some people like the extra sourness that a longer-proofed dough creates and the texture it produces. Neither of these is nominally "wrong"; what I would recommend is finding the sweet spot for you and your family and how you prefer your dough and your bread to be.

Troubleshooting Doughs & FAQ

I receive many questions about dough, including those listed here, but there is a key question I always ask in return: How do your loaves bake?

If you are making loaves of baked sourdough that you are very happy with and enjoy eating, my advice is always the same: Do not worry about how the dough behaves. All that matters here is the baked outcome.

If you feel that your doughs and loaves need tweaking, these are some of the typical questions that I am asked, along with my responses.

Why has my dough not risen?

There are key reasons that dough does not rise. First, your starter may be weak; see page 20 for guidance on how to fix these issues.

Second, if it has been cold overnight, the dough will take longer to fully proof and needs to be allowed more time. Refer to pages 47–49 about underproofed dough for more tips.

Or if it is a dough made with whole-grain flours, or with added extras, it will be heavier and will not grow as much as others but will bake to a great loaf.

Why is my dough sticky?

Sticky dough can be the result of the flours you have used in the dough; for example, rye or einkorn flour, in which case this is normal.

Underproofed dough can be sticky and stiff; allow it longer to proof. Overproofed dough will be very sticky and sloppy, even liquid if it has overproofed to the extreme. Refer to the sections about under- and overproofed dough (pages 47–52) for more help.

Why does my dough not come away clean from the bowl like yours does?

Your dough does not need to look and behave like mine; if it does not come away from the bowl cleanly, it does not mean it is not a good dough. If the resultant loaf did not bake well, refer to the previous questions. I use glass bowls; sometimes dough sticks more to bowls made of other materials and that could be all that is making the difference. If a lot of dough is sticking to the bowl, the dough may be overly sticky; refer to the "Sticky Doughs" section (page 53) for tips.

Why does my dough not come into a ball?

Again, the dough does not need to come into a ball to be a successful dough. In fact, different flours and handling may mean it will not come into a ball. All that being said, ensure that you are doing the pulls and folds with enough emphasis to build the structure of your dough well and give it the best chance to come into a ball.

Why is my dough not bubbly after the main proof?

Doughs do not need to be bubbly; they look enticing, but the fact is that bubbly doughs actually tend to indicate the dough is overproofed.

If your dough has a few bubbles and a smooth, upwardly domed surface, it is nicely proofed.

If your dough is flat and has not grown but has random bubbles, it is underproofed and trying hard to grow more, but it lacks the power to do so. If your dough is very bubbly, soft and dipping down into the bowl, it is overproofed.

Why does my dough spread when I turn it out of the banneton?

The dough will spread if it is too wet and therefore needs less water from the start. It will also spread if you did not give the dough enough tension when you pulled it together to go into the banneton, or if the dough overproofed.

Why do we need to score the dough before baking?

Scoring dough encourages your loaf to grow as it bakes. Unscored dough will still grow as it bakes, but it will not grow as much as it could, and it will probably crack anyway, so by scoring it, you choose how it grows and how the crust opens.

Why am I unable to score my dough?

If your dough cannot be scored cleanly and successfully, either replace the blade you are using or ensure that the dough is not too soft, which can be the case if a dough is overproofed or sticky from needing less water from the start. This can also happen if the dough did not have enough tension when it was pulled together for the banneton. If your dough is too soft, it will be difficult to score it successfully. Refer to the "Sticky Doughs" section (page 53), or previous questions for other suggestions.

Why does my dough deflate when I score it?

Doughs often deflate when scored; the key is how they then bake. If they rise and bake well, there is nothing to be concerned about. If they deflate and then bake to a flat, spread loaf, the dough may have overproofed, or needs to be stronger, and many of the previous questions and answers and the dough discussion from the "All About Dough" section, starting on page 45, will help.

Why does my dough stick to the banneton?

Dough may stick to the banneton for two key reasons:

- If the banneton does not have a layer of rice flour inside it to prevent sticking, or the layer is not thick enough. See page 30 for how to prepare bannetons with rice flour.

- If the dough is too wet as a result of too much water in the dough or overproofing. See pages 51 and 53 for more information.

Why does my dough not rise in the fridge?

Dough does not need to rise in the fridge, only in the oven. The aim of the time in the fridge is to firm up the dough so that when you turn it out to score and bake it, it does not spread.

Do I need to use a smaller pan to hold my dough?

Your dough should have sufficient structure built into it from all of your work doing pulls and folds, the time in the fridge and using good flour to hold its own shape when you turn it out to bake it. However, if you find that even with all of the tips and help in this section, you still struggle to create a firm dough, then try using a smaller pan or a loaf pan to give the dough shape while it bakes.

Can I halve your recipes?

Yes, you can scale my recipes up or down to whatever size you would like them to be. Apply the fraction or percentage that you want to use to each quantity of the ingredients, use a banneton and pan suitable for the size and amend the baking time accordingly.

For example, to halve the standard My Master Recipe made with strong white bread flour:

Convert:

50 g (¼ cup) starter

350 g (1½ cups) water

500 g (4 cups) strong white bread flour

7 g (1 tsp) salt

to:

25 g (⅛ cup) starter

175 g (¾ cup) water

250 g (2 cups) strong white bread flour

3.5 g (½ tsp) salt

Use a smaller banneton and bake for 30 to 35 minutes, or until browned to your liking.

How many pulls and folds are needed for each set?

There is no fixed answer to this. The first set will need more than the rest—I aim for 20 to 25—then after that, a lot less are required. The dough will tell you itself once you have done enough, as it will come into a tight ball and you will struggle to do any more. That is when you can stop until the next set.

What if I do not have time to do all of the sets of pulls and folds?

In an ideal world, it would be beneficial to your dough to be able to complete all the sets of pulls and folds as laid out in my recipes. But as we know, life is not always ideal, and sometimes we do not have all that time, so as an alternative to doing three or four sets of pulls and folds, mix your dough to a ragged mix, cover it, allow it to sit on the counter for 30 to 60 minutes and then perform one longer single round of pulls and folds. Do this for 5 minutes continuously to build up the dough. Then, cover the bowl and leave it to proof per the recipe.

The dough will be looser, and there is every chance that the loaf will be a little flatter, as the dough may spread a little when you turn it out from the banneton. However, it will still bake to a good loaf, and can easily be done this way anytime you are short on time.

If you are concerned that the dough is looser and softer than usual, bake it in a loaf pan instead, per the Master Recipe Sandwich Loaf (page 77).

Troubleshooting Baked Loaves & FAQ

There is no single way that baked sourdough loaves "should" look; it can be very easy to believe that they should look a certain way. I hope that I can reassure you that they do not need to be holey, or have big open scores, or look like round beach balls. Every sourdough loaf will look different based on the flours used to make them, how the dough is handled and how they are baked. They will all be unique.

If you do have concerns, these are questions that I am typically asked.

Why is my loaf flat?

A flat loaf will be the result of underproofed dough, overproofed dough or a dough that was too wet. Refer to pages 45–51 for help.

It can also be the result of not pulling the dough together tightly enough when it was being pulled together to go into the banneton.

Why does my loaf have large, uneven holes?

Large, uneven holes inside a loaf are a result of the dough being underproofed and not being able to rise and lift fully and evenly as it is baked.

Why is my loaf a bit flat but with a peak in the middle?

This is also a result of the dough being underproofed or having a weak starter. The loaf has tried to rise, but has not had the power to manage it all over.

Why has my loaf not got an "ear"?

"Ears" occur when dough is scored and the baked loaf splits and produces a wave with a risen crest. Ears look impressive, but are not a necessity, and loaves without ears are not in any way failures.

Ears are the result of a strong powerful dough and how the dough is scored. To encourage an ear, score your dough off center, hold the blade at a 45-degree angle and score ⅜ inch (1 cm) deep. See the section on how to shape dough for an oval loaf (page 43) for photographic guidance.

Why have my scores closed up?

Scores close up if the dough is too soft due to being too wet or overproofed, or if you do not score deeply enough. Aim to score firmly, ⅜ inch (1 cm) deep, when scoring dough.

Why does my loaf have bumpy edges?

If your dough was very soft when it was turned into your pan for baking, it can become indented by the parchment paper lining your pan, giving your loaf dented, bumpy cooked edges. Refer to pages 51 and 53 for how to fix very soft doughs. Alternatively, scrunch up your parchment paper before using it, to "soften" it, then lay it inside your pan, pushing it out to fill the space.

The crust is too hard; how do I soften it?

To soften the crust, once the loaf is fully baked, wrap it in a clean tea towel and place it on a wire rack to cool. The fabric will trap the steam and soften the crust. Or refer to "The Softer Sourdough Collection" chapter (page 115) for more ideas.

I prefer less holey bread. How can I make a loaf with a tighter crumb?

To produce a tighter crumb in loaves, follow the recipes in "The Softer Sourdough Collection" chapter (page 115), using milk or oil in the dough. Or include whole wheat or whole-grain flour in the dough, which produces a denser dough and thus a tighter crumb.

How do you store your bread?

Once the loaf is baked and before slicing into it, I leave it on a wire rack to cool; this can be anywhere from 3 hours minimum up to 24 hours. The loaf remains crusty and perfectly fresh. Once the loaf has been sliced, I store it in reusable plastic bread bags. The crust softens, but the loaf remains soft.

How can I make my bread crusty again after it has softened?

To restore a crunch to your crust, heat your oven to 350°F (180°C), place your loaf on a baking sheet, sprinkle it lightly with water and heat it in the oven for 5 to 10 minutes. As it cools, it will become even crustier.

How do you freeze sourdough loaves?

Once the loaf is baked and placed on a wire rack to cool, leave it to cool completely. This may take several hours. Once it is completely cooled, wrap it in a bag or the covering of your choice and place it in the freezer. To defrost, take the loaf from the freezer, remove the bag or cover and place the loaf on a wire rack completely uncovered. Allow it several hours to fully defrost, and it will be like a new loaf, perfectly crusty and ready to eat.

Why is my loaf gummy inside?

Gummy loaves can be the result of cutting into a fresh loaf too early, not baking the loaf for long enough, a proofing issue or too much water in your dough. The best way to establish what your issue is to systematically eliminate each possibility—was the dough underproofed, overproofed or too wet? These would all produce a gummy loaf. Or it could be as simple as whether the loaf cooked enough. If the loaf is very pale, try baking longer next time.

My loaves keep having a very hard or burned base. How can I prevent that?

Hard or overcooked bases are the result of uneven heat in your oven. One way to stop it from happening is to place foil inside your pan, underneath the dough, and parchment paper. Another option is to place a baking or cookie sheet on a rack farther down the oven to drive the heat away from the bottom of your pan and evenly distribute the heat around the oven.

Can I make your master recipe as an oval instead of round? Does it change the time it needs to bake?

Yes, you can use my recipes and bake them in whatever shape you choose: round, oval, sandwich loaf, Bundt pan—you can use the same recipes with whatever you have on hand. The recipes in this book will provide guidance and timings. To make my full-size master recipes as an oval instead of round, the baking time will not change.

Do you really have to wait for over an hour before slicing freshly baked loaves?

Yes, you do. It is so tempting to cut into a warm, steaming loaf, but initially the loaf is still finishing baking; plus, if you cut into it too soon, the steam will fill the inside of the loaf and make it gummy. It really is worth the wait, and the bread stays warm for a long time, so you can still enjoy some warmth without ruining the loaf by waiting for more than an hour. The only time you do not need to wait is when baking rolls, ciabatta, baguettes or other smaller breads.

ALL ABOUT TIMING

It is very easy with bread dough, particularly sourdough, to feel that the dough is fully in control and that you are forever at its whim. A fear factor that comes with making sourdough can make people feel that it is calling all the shots, as if you must jump to its tune, but I am here to tell you that this is categorically not the case. You do not ever need to get up at 3:00 a.m. to manage your dough (yes, I have known people who do that); you can control the timings and readiness of your dough. Read on to learn how.

How to Manipulate the Sourdough-Making Process

In this section, my aim is to provide you with the tips to be able to manage and control your doughs as you need to. These tips are all based on my standard master recipe timetable (page 61).

Extend It

If you would like to lengthen the time it will take for your dough to fully proof, whether to fit it around life events or to experiment and see how the extra time develops the flavor of your dough, reduce the amount of starter you use in your dough by half to extend the main bulk proof. Follow the process as is written, but allow for the longer proof time. This could mean allow 5 to 6 more hours for proofing (depending on the room temperature). As always, watch the dough in this scenario to see when it has fully proofed.

Or lengthen the time once the fully proofed dough is in the banneton by leaving it in the fridge for up to 24 hours, then bake as usual. You can even experiment with leaving the dough for longer than 24 hours; the only time this will negatively affect the outcome is if the dough is not strong enough to withstand the extra time.

You will know whether that was the case if your dough flattens and spreads when you come to bake it and does not lift in the oven.

Or do both! By extending both proofs, you may find that you prefer the timing and the outcome.

Shorten It

If you would like to make the whole process shorter, either use the Same Day Timetable (page 62), or once the dough is in the banneton, cover and place it in the freezer for 30 to 45 minutes to replace the fridge time in the standard recipe.

When you are ready to bake, take the dough from the freezer, turn it out, score it and bake as usual. Do not allow it to warm up; this will defeat the objective of the time in the cold temperature.

Halt It

For this job, the fridge is your friend. The cold puts dough to sleep, as the yeast activation slows down significantly in lower temperatures.

- If life steps in and you suddenly cannot continue with the process at that time, place your bowl of dough, covered, in the fridge.

- If you started the dough early in the day and realize that the overnight or main bulk proof will now be too long and risks overproofing or would mean your needing to get up at 2:00 a.m. to complete the next step, place the covered bowl of dough in the fridge.

- If it is warmer in your kitchen than you initially realized and your dough is, or is at risk of, growing too fast, place the covered bowl in the fridge.

In each situation, when you are ready to continue, remove the bowl from the fridge, leave it covered on the counter for an hour to warm up again and continue from the point at which you had left it.

Protect It

If your ambient or room temperature is going to be a lot higher than 71°F (22°C) during the overnight or main bulk proof, it will be at risk of overproofing if left to proof for more than 3 to 4 hours. Either plan ahead and follow the hot temperatures timetable on page 63 or, if you would still like to proof on the counter overnight, use less starter in your dough. This is the perfect antidote to hot temperatures and overproofing. Less starter means that the dough proofs much slower; use 20 grams (scant ⅛ cup) of starter only, making no other changes to the rest of the ingredients.

If, as a result of using this smaller amount of starter, your dough is not as proofed as you would like the next morning, allow it longer to fully proof. It is a lot easier to give underproofed dough more time to fully proof than to undo overproofing.

Boost It

If you would like to speed things up or give your dough a boost, the amount of starter teamed with room temperature are the tools.

- If you would like to force your dough to proof faster, follow the elements of the Same Day Timetable (page 62). This includes using more starter in the dough and proofing it in a warm environment.

- If it is winter and your dough is struggling to proof well overnight in the cold temperatures, use an increased amount of starter. The warmth of your kitchen plus the extra starter will give the dough a kickstart in growth before the temperatures drop. Alternatively, place the dough in a warm place in between the pulls and folds to encourage an initial growth, before then placing it on the counter overnight. Placing the dough in your oven with the pilot light on would be ideal, but do not forget about it—remember to remove it before going to bed.

- If the recipe states to use 50 grams (¼ cup) of starter, use 100 grams (½ cup) instead and reduce the amount of water or other liquid by 25 grams (⅛ cup).

- Another way to give the dough an initial boost is by using warm water when you first mix the dough. Water at 100°F (38°C) is ideal.

Making and Baking Timetables

The following timetables provide a selection of timing options. They can be used as a guideline for making any of the recipes in the book, as well as the basis for creating your own recipe.

My Typical Master Recipe Timetable

This is the typical timetable that I work to whenever I bake. The steps refer to the steps in the recipes. The timings are a guide only and do not have to be exact.

1. 9:00 a.m.: Take your starter from the fridge and leave it on the counter with its lid firmly on.

2. 11:00 a.m.: Feed your starter per your recipe requirements. Cover and allow it to become active.

3. 5:00 p.m., Step 1: Mix together all the ingredients.

4. 6:00 p.m., Step 2: Complete the first set of pulls and folds.

5. 7:00 to 9:00 p.m., Step 3: Complete three more sets of pulls and folds.

6. 9:00 p.m., Step 4: Leave the covered bowl on the counter overnight.

7. 7:00 a.m., Step 5: Pull the dough together, place it in the banneton, cover and put it into the fridge. (May be later if the dough needs longer to fully proof.)

8. 10:00 a.m. onward, Step 6: Bake directly from the fridge.

Workday Master Recipe Timetable

The aim of this timetable is to allow you to be able to fit making a full master recipe dough around your working day. The steps refer to the steps in the recipes.

1. Feed your starter direct from the fridge, either the night before you want to use it or first thing in the morning before work, and leave it on the counter with its lid firmly on. Do not leave it anywhere too warm. The starter will not need to be fed again unless it has become thin and inactive. Or refer to the alternative ways to use your starter on pages 21–23.

2. Once home from work, Step 1: Mix together all the ingredients.

3. After an hour, Step 2: Complete the first set of pulls and folds.

4. After an hour, Step 3: Complete two or three more sets of pulls and folds as time allows before going to bed.

5. Bedtime, Step 4: Leave the covered bowl on the counter overnight.

6. Before work the next morning, Step 5: Pull the dough together, place it in the banneton, cover and put into the fridge.

7. In the evening after work, Step 6: Bake directly from the fridge.

Same Day Timetable

This timetable enables you to make and bake a loaf within a day. The steps refer to the steps in the recipe; for the full details of a same-day bake, visit "The Same Day Collection" starting on page 175.

1. Feed your starter the night before you will make your dough. Or refer to the alternative ways to use your starter on pages 21–23.

2. 9:30 a.m., Step 1: Complete the first rough mix of all your ingredients.

3. 10:00 a.m., Step 2: Perform the first set of pulls and folds and place the covered bowl in a warm place.

4. 10:30 a.m., Step 3: Perform the next set of pulls and folds. Place the covered bowl back in the warmth.

5. 11:00 a.m., Step 4: Perform the last set of pulls and folds. Place the covered bowl back in the warmth.

6. 2:00 p.m., Step 5: Pull the dough together for the banneton and place it in the fridge.

7. 5:00 p.m., Step 6: Bake directly from the fridge.

Morning Bake Timetable

This timetable is designed for you to be able to bake your loaf ready for breakfast. The steps refer to the steps in my recipes.

1. 9:00 a.m.: Take your starter from the fridge and leave it on the counter with its lid firmly on.

2. 11:00 a.m.: Feed your starter per your recipe requirements. Cover and allow it to become active.

3. 5:00 p.m., Step 1: Mix together all the ingredients.

4. 6:00 p.m., Step 2: Complete the first set of pulls and folds.

5. 7:00 to 9:00 p.m., Step 3: Complete three more sets of pulls and folds.

6. 9:00 p.m., Step 4: Leave the covered bowl on the counter overnight.

7. 7:00 a.m., Step 5: Pull the dough together, place it in the banneton, cover and put in the fridge. (May be later if the dough needs longer to fully proof.)

8. Step 6: You have three choices for this step: Place the banneton of dough in the freezer for 30 to 45 minutes, then bake directly from the freezer. Or leave the dough in the banneton in the fridge all day and bake that night. Leave the freshly baked loaf on a rack, uncovered, all night to cool; it will be ready to eat in the morning. Or leave the dough in the banneton all day and night in the fridge, and bake directly from the fridge the next morning.

Hot Places or Temperatures Timetable

This timetable is designed for you to be able to manage making sourdough in warm temperatures, particularly useful in hot summers or in locations that are hot all year round. The key to this timetable is watching your dough in the heat.

1. Feed your starter the night before you will make your dough.

2. 9:30 a.m., Step 1: Complete the first rough mix of all your ingredients.

3. 10:00 a.m., Step 2: Perform the first set of pulls and folds.

4. 10:30 a.m., Step 3: Perform the next set of pulls and folds.

5. 11:00 a.m., Step 4: Perform the last set of pulls and folds. Leave the covered bowl on your counter until you see the dough double in size.

6. Once the dough has doubled in size, Step 5: Pull the dough together for the banneton and place it into the fridge.

7. Next day, Step 6: Bake directly from the fridge the next morning.

How to Create Your Own Timetable

There are certain fixed stages in the sourdough process, and as long as these stages happen, the starting and finishing points can be moved around as you need them to; it is far more flexible than you may have thought. Think of the whole process as a fixed segment of your clock that you can move all the way around, meaning that you can move the start time to any time on the clock face; all that needs to be planned for is for the dough to have enough time to fully proof.

If you break it down, these are the stages of making sourdough once your starter is ready to use:

Stage 1: the first rough mix of all of the ingredients

Stage 2: letting the mix sit for an hour

Stage 3: completing the sets of pulls and folds, typically across the next 3 to 4 hours

Stage 4: leaving the dough to bulk proof

Stage 5: moving the dough to the banneton

Stage 6: cold proofing the dough

Stage 7: baking

The length of time needed to complete the whole process depends on Stages 4 and 6, and these can be amended and managed based on the tips on pages 60 and 61.

Once you have that understanding, you can work to timetables of your own creation, making them as long or short as you need to on the day.

If you want a loaf to be ready at a certain time of day, work backward from the end point of the timetable to determine when to begin your dough.

How to Amend Recipes for Your Personal Preference

As with the timings, recipes in this book can be tweaked for your personal preference. For example, I prefer small amounts of salt in my bread; you may prefer more. The dough will not suffer if you use more salt than I do.

You may prefer more or less of the additional ingredients in a dough than I use; again, please tweak them to suit your choices. Just keep in mind that if you overload sourdough with too many extras, such as cheese or seeds, the dough will be heavier and will not grow as much during baking. That is not to say it will not still taste great, though!

In the following chapters, you will also see how my recipes can be converted to bigger or smaller loaves, or baked in different pans or shapes. The fact is that the possibilities are endless, and once you are conversant with how your starter works and dough behaves, the baked outcome can be whatever you choose for it to be regarding size, shape and look.

In "The Master Recipe Sourdough Collection" chapter (page 71) of this book, you will see how my standard "master recipe," which is the basis of all of my sourdough creations, can be changed and adapted. You will find that the recipe can be used for round or oval loaves, and other versions and uses of the recipe converted for making smaller loaves, simple wedge rolls, sandwich pan loaves and Pullman pan loaves. These recipes can be a guide to show how any of the recipes in the book can be made bigger, smaller, as rolls or baked for a different shape. "The Shaped Collection" chapter (page 159) shows more ways that the dough can be manipulated to create different looks.

You can also very simply convert any of the recipes to make them smaller or bigger. A standard full-size master recipe loaf can be converted to a baby master loaf by multiplying every ingredient quantity by 0.6 and baking for 5 to 10 minutes less.

A baby loaf can be scaled back up to a full-size loaf by multiplying all the ingredient quantities by 1.67 and baking the loaf for 5 to 10 minutes longer.

Choices of Pans for Baking

Sourdough can be many things, not just a round, crusty loaf. The dough can be used to make any shape or type of bread you would like.

Consequently, the loaf recipes in this book can be baked as free form or in a pan of some sort. The recipes show loaves made in different shapes and forms, and each one can be swapped. For example, the dough for My Master Recipe (page 33) can be baked as a free-form boule as shown, or in a pan per the Master Recipe Sandwich Loaf (page 77) by making the dough from the recipe from Steps 1 through 4, then following the process for making the sandwich loaf (page 77) from Step 5 onward.

Alternatively, the dough can be used to produce a Pullman loaf by using a Pullman loaf pan and following the recipe from Step 5 onward as shown on page 84, to make a decorative loaf by using a Bundt pan from Step 5 onward as shown on page 81, or baking in a wide, flat sheet pan as focaccia as shown on page 148. These are just a few examples, and the recipes later in the book provide many other options. I would also suggest experimenting with any other pans you have in your kitchen.

Tips for Batch Baking

When I make numerous loaves at once, I use a single bowl per dough, even if every dough I am making is identical. I do this for one single reason: I would need a HUGE bowl for a dough that is double or triple the normal size to fully proof.

However, if you do have such a bowl and would like to make double, triple or larger quantities, follow all of the usual steps of the recipe, then split the dough after the main or overnight bulk proof to place it into your bannetons or pans, whichever you are using, for the second proof prior to baking.

Another reason I use a single bowl per dough is to watch and manage the growth of the dough and to keep the dough manageable for my small hands.

Making multiple doughs with my recipes is truly straightforward; it is as simple as doubling or tripling the quantities, however much you need. And if you do want to double or triple my master recipe, feed your starter double or triple the usual amounts to generate the amount of active starter you will need to make your doughs. So, if you need 50 grams (¼ cup) for one dough, double it for two doughs, triple it for three and so on.

Please note that you do not need to begin with more starter for it to be able make more; just feed your usual base amount for the job and it will work perfectly.

Splitting a Single Dough for Two or More Bakes

If you would like to make a single standard master recipe dough and split it to be able to make two or more loaves, a good time to split it is after the main bulk proof. Follow the recipe up to and including the main or overnight proof, then at the point of putting the dough into your banneton(s) or pan(s) at Step 5, split it into the number of doughs that you need. Use the same handling to pull the pieces into shape, place the doughs into your bannetons or pans and continue with the steps of the recipe.

Cold Baking

Baking your bread from a cold oven start sounds counterintuitive. We have been trained to believe that ovens should be searingly hot before we put our carefully tended dough into them to bake.

I can tell you absolutely that that is not the case. Every loaf as well as most of the nonloaves in this book has been baked from a cold start, as well as tested in a preheated oven. You will find full details in each recipe.

You can also apply my cold baking methods to any of the recipes in my previous book, *Whole Grain Sourdough at Home*, or experiment using other bread recipes to see what the outcome is.

How It Works

When you put the dough into the cold oven and then turn it on, as the oven warms up, the dough receives an extra proofing boost before it then bakes. Often loaves baked from a cold start grow more in size than those baked in a preheated oven.

I am often asked whether the baking time includes the time it takes for the oven to come up to temperature *plus* the baking time. The answer is no. For example, if I bake my standard-sized loaves from a cold start, the loaf is in the oven for a total of 55 minutes from the time that I place the pan full of dough in the oven and switch the oven on, whereas I bake the same-sized loaves in a preheated oven for 50 minutes total.

The key benefit of baking from a cold start is that it saves time, power and therefore money. But it also removes stress and planning; you do not need to remember to preheat your oven or plan ahead; you can just put the pan of dough in the oven, switch it on and go.

For me, that saves 20 minutes of time for the oven to heat up; for others, it may be longer.

The only time that cold baking might not work tends to be if the oven is older, and even then it might just take longer to fully bake.

How to Bake from a Cold Start

The process is truly simple: At the point when you want to bake, place your cold dough in your cold pan in your cold oven. Then, turn the oven on to the required temperature for that recipe. Turn a timer to the total time given in the recipe and bake. No planning, no juggling hot pans, no wasted time or power.

I am often asked, "I have baked my loaf from a cold start and I have got another one to bake; do I need to wait for the oven to cool down to start again?"

The answer is no; if your oven has already been on, bake exactly per the recipe, at the same temperature, but follow the time for the preheated oven, usually 5 to 10 minutes less. No other amendments are needed.

Part 2

THE RECIPES

In this section of the book, I am excited to bring you a selection of recipes that I have loved developing. These include using my master recipe to create differently sized and shaped loaves; adding new flavors and textures to the dough; using the dough to create different types of bread; and using your starter for different bakes . . . the possibilities are truly endless, and my struggle has only been knowing when to stop. I hope you will try many and love them all.

Sourdough offers so many options; whatever breads you would like to make, you can make them with a sourdough starter. I hope my recipes show you how and inspire you in your kitchen.

Except for "The Same Day Collection" chapter (page 175), all the recipes are based on using my standard timetable for making the dough; however, they can all be made to alternative timetables, all of which you will find in the "All About Timing" section (page 60).

THE MASTER RECIPE
Sourdough Collection

In this collection, you will find my master recipe converted to be able to make loaves in different sizes and shapes. These are all derivatives of My Master Recipe (page 33) to show how the main recipe can be used to create other loaves or rolls based on what your household prefers or fancies.

Whatever you want your sourdough to be—full-sized loaves, baby loaves, sandwich, square or shaped loaves—you will find how to achieve that with My Master Recipe as your base. This one recipe can be your sourdough foundation.

Baby Master Loaf

This loaf is a scaled-down version of My Master Recipe (page 33). This is a great size if you prefer smaller loaves or want to experiment with making loaves using less flour or different flours, or including new additions. For this loaf, I use a smaller banneton as listed to the side. With smaller doughs, it is often easier to begin the process using a spatula or bowl scraper to first mix the dough.

PREP: Feed your starter to generate the 30 grams (⅛ cup) of active starter needed for the recipe; see page 18 for full details. Prepare a round banneton, 6¾ inches (17 cm) in diameter and 3¼ inches (8.5 cm) deep, or a lined bowl, with rice flour, and set aside a medium-sized baking pan with a lid, plus parchment paper.

Makes 1 small loaf

30 g (⅛ cup) active starter

210 g (¾ cup plus 2 tbsp) water

300 g (2½ cups) strong white bread flour

4 g (½ tsp) salt, or to taste

Rice flour, for dusting

Step 1: In the early evening, in a large mixing bowl, roughly mix together all the ingredients, except the rice flour, until you have a shaggy, rough dough. Cover the bowl with a clean shower cap or your choice of cover and leave the bowl on the counter for 1 hour.

Step 2: After an hour or so, perform the first set of pulls and folds until the dough feels less sticky and comes together into a soft ball. Cover the bowl again and leave it on your counter.

Step 3: Over the next few hours, do three more sets of pulls and folds on the dough, covering the dough after each set. Perform the final set before going to bed.

Step 4: Leave the covered bowl on the counter overnight, typically 8 to 10 hours, at 64 to 68°F (18 to 20°C).

Step 5: In the morning, you should be greeted by a bowl full of grown dough. Perform one last set of pulls and folds to form the dough into a nice ball. Place your hand over the whole dough and lift it into the banneton, smooth side down. Sprinkle extra rice flour down the sides and over the top of the dough. Cover the banneton and place it in the fridge for 3 to 24 hours.

Step 6: When you are ready to bake, decide whether you would like to bake in a preheated oven or from a cold start. If preheating, set the oven to 425°F (220°C) convection or 450°F (230°C) conventional.

Remove the cover from the banneton, then place the parchment paper over the top of the banneton and the pan upside down over the top of them both. With one hand under the banneton and one on the pan, turn it all over together to turn the dough out of the banneton and into the pan. Score the dome of dough.

If you preheated the oven, put the lid on the pan and bake for 40 minutes. If using a cold start, place the covered pan of dough in the oven, set the temperature as directed and set a timer for 45 minutes.

After the baking time, remove the pan from the oven. Open the lid and check the loaf. If you feel that it is looking pale, place the pan with the loaf back in the hot oven, minus the lid, for 5 to 10 minutes to brown the loaf to the color of your choice.

Step 7: Once baked, carefully remove the loaf from the pan, saving the parchment paper for next time, and allow the baked loaf to cool on a wire rack for at least an hour before slicing.

Baby Master Wedge Rolls

These rolls are made using my Baby Master Loaf recipe (page 72) as the base and cutting the dough into wedge sections prior to baking. This is the simplest, most hands-off way that I use for making sourdough rolls. The same process can be used with any of my recipes, amending the baking time slightly if using a larger dough or cutting bigger wedges. You can apply this method for making rolls to any of the dough recipes in this book. With smaller doughs, it is often easier to begin the process using a spatula or bowl scraper to first mix the dough.

PREP: Feed your starter to generate the 30 grams (⅛ cup) of active starter needed for the recipe; see page 18 for full details. Prepare a round banneton, 6¾ inches (17 cm) in diameter and 3¼ inches (8.5 cm) deep, or a lined bowl, with rice flour, and set aside a large baking or cookie sheet, plus parchment paper.

Makes 6 wedge rolls

30 g (⅛ cup) active starter

210 g (¾ cup plus 2 tbsp) water

300 g (2½ cups) strong white bread flour, plus more for dusting

4 g (½ tsp) salt, or to taste

Rice flour, for dusting

Step 1: In the early evening, in a large mixing bowl, roughly mix together all the ingredients, except the rice flour, until you have a shaggy, rough dough. Cover the bowl with a clean shower cap or your choice of cover and leave the bowl on the counter for 1 hour.

Step 2: After an hour or so, perform the first set of pulls and folds until the dough feels less sticky and comes together into a soft ball. Cover the bowl again and leave it on your counter.

Step 3: Over the next few hours, do three more sets of pulls and folds on the dough, covering the dough after each set. Perform the final set before going to bed.

Step 4: Leave the covered bowl on the counter overnight, typically 8 to 10 hours, at 64 to 68°F (18 to 20°C).

Step 5: In the morning, your bowl should be full of happy, bouncy dough with a smooth surface. Perform one final set of pulls and folds, once around the bowl, to pull the dough into a loose but still bouncy ball. Carefully lift the dough and place it, smooth side down, in the banneton, adding extra rice flour down the sides and across the top of the dough to prevent sticking. Cover the banneton with the same shower cap and place it in the fridge. Leave the dough in the fridge for at least 3 hours, or a maximum of 24.

Step 6: When you are ready to bake, decide whether you would like to bake in a preheated oven or from a cold start. If preheating, set the oven to 400°F (200°C) convection or 425°F (220°C) conventional.

Remove the cover from the banneton and turn the dough out gently onto a lightly floured counter.

Using a nonstick dough knife, a bench scraper or a sharp kitchen knife, cut the dough into six equal wedges. Gently place the wedges on the prepared pan. They grow as they bake, so allow some space between them, but if they do bake and kiss during the process, you can separate them later.

Step 7: Bake the rolls, uncovered, in the preheated oven for 18 to 20 minutes, or until nicely risen and starting to brown. To bake from a cold start, place the baking sheet in the oven, set the temperature as directed and bake uncovered for a total of 18 to 22 minutes, or until nicely risen and browning.

Step 8: Once baked, remove the rolls from the oven and allow to cool slightly before eating.

*See step-by-step pictures on the next page.

Top Tip:
These rolls freeze and defrost perfectly; I make them in batches and always have some available in my freezer. Allow them to fully cool before wrapping them in a bag or placing them in a freezer-proof container, and freeze. To defrost, place the rolls, uncovered, on a wire rack; they will defrost fully in 2 to 3 hours.

Baby Master Wedge Rolls (Continued)

Follow the steps to make your dough, all the way to proofing it in the fridge.

When you are ready to bake, gently turn the dough out onto a floured surface.

Using a nonstick dough knife or sharp knife, cut the dough into six even-sized wedges.

Place the wedges onto a prepared oven tray and bake as per the recipe.

Master Recipe Sandwich Loaf

This version of My Master Recipe (page 33) allows you to make the same bread, but bake it in a loaf pan to create a sandwich loaf. The slices will then fit into a toaster. This dough has more water than the standard free-form recipe, which creates a lively, bouncy dough. Baking in a loaf pan tends to produce a loaf with a tighter crumb, which means it is less "holey" than other loaves; this also makes it more user-friendly for sandwiches and stops the butter from falling through the holes.

PREP: Feed your starter to generate the 50 grams (¼ cup) of active starter needed for the recipe; see page 18 for full details. Line a 2-pound (900-g) loaf pan (9 x 5 inches [23 x 14 cm]) or an 8-inch (20-cm) round pan with a liner or parchment paper.

Makes 1 standard loaf

50 g (¼ cup) active starter

375 g (1½ cups plus 2 tbsp) water

500 g (4 cups) strong white bread flour

7 g (1 tsp) salt, or to taste

Step 1: In the early evening, in a medium-sized or large mixing bowl, roughly mix together all the ingredients until you have a sticky, rough dough. Cover the bowl with a clean shower cap or your choice of cover and leave the bowl on the counter for 1 hour.

Step 2: After an hour or so, perform the first set of pulls and folds until the dough feels less sticky. The dough will become easily stretchy and come into a soft ball; at that point stop. Cover the bowl again and leave it on your counter.

Step 3: Over the next few hours, do three more sets of pulls and folds on the dough—the dough will be nicely stretchy and bouncy—covering the dough again after each set. Perform the final set before going to bed.

Step 4: Leave the covered bowl on the counter overnight, typically 8 to 10 hours, at 64 to 68°F (18 to 20°C).

Step 5: In the morning, the dough will have grown to double, maybe even triple in size; it will be a bouncy dough. Have your desired pan ready and place the paper liner on the counter. Gently lift and fold small handfuls of dough from one side of the bowl into the middle in a line, using the same pulling and folding action as used previously. Turn the bowl 180 degrees and do the same on the other side so that you have a thick sausage of dough in the middle of the bowl.

(continued)

Master Recipe Sandwich Loaf (Continued)

With a wetted hand, place your whole hand over the dough, turn the bowl upside down and gently ease the dough from the bowl into your hand. Place the dough, seam side down, on the paper and slip your hand out from underneath the dough. Use the paper to lift the dough into the pan, cover it with the same shower cap and leave it on the counter.

Note:

The dough will be lively and may "splodge" onto the paper, which will be fine—it will fill the pan and regain its shape during the final proof.

Allow the dough to proof again, letting it grow level with the edge of the pan and just peek over the top. This may take 2 to 3 hours, depending on the temperature of your kitchen. The surface will become smooth and the dough will spread to fill the pan.

Step 6: When you are ready to bake, decide whether you would like to bake in a preheated oven or from a cold start. If preheating, set the oven to 350°F (180°C) convection or 400°F (200°C) conventional.

If you preheated the oven, bake uncovered for 40 minutes. If using a cold start, place the uncovered pan of dough in the oven, set the temperature as directed and set a timer for 45 minutes.

Step 7: Remove the loaf from the oven and the pan, remove the paper, tap the base of the loaf and if it sounds hollow, the loaf is baked. If not, return it to the oven, out of the pan, directly onto the rack to bake for a further 5 to 10 minutes. Remove from the oven and allow it to cool on a wire rack for at least an hour before slicing.

*See step-by-step pictures on the next page.

After the overnight proof, have a loaf tin and liner/parchment paper ready.

To place the dough into the pan, pull the dough across itself in a line.

Turn the bowl right round, 180 degrees, and pull the dough across itself again in a line to make a thick sausage of dough.

Lift, and place the dough, smooth side up, onto the paper; use the paper to lift the dough into the pan.

Cover, and leave on the counter to proof again.

Once the dough has grown and fills the pan, bake as per the recipe.

Master Recipe Bundt Pan Loaf

This loaf and the accompanying photo are very special to me; this was the loaf I made to celebrate my 50th birthday. I love savory flavors, and for me, a celebration meal is full of savory selections, so to celebrate my birthday, this was my choice! A celebration sourdough loaf. I also love how it shows that bread, including sourdough, can come in any shape or size. To slice and serve this loaf, I slice it like a Bundt cake, cutting thin wedges of bread; this produces slices with a lot of really crunchy crust and a soft interior. These can be eaten fresh or fit easily into your toaster.

PREP: Feed your starter to generate the 100 grams (½ cup) of active starter needed for the recipe; see page 18 for details. Prepare a 12-cup (2.8-L) Bundt pan, 10½ inches (26.7 cm) in diameter and 4½ inches (11.5 cm) deep. If your pan is nonstick, no further prep is needed; if not, sprinkle it with rice flour throughout the interior.

Makes 1 standard loaf

100 g (½ cup) active starter

325 g (1¼ cups) water

500 g (4 cups) strong white bread flour

7 g (1 tsp) salt, or to taste

Step 1: In the early evening, in a large mixing bowl, roughly mix together all the ingredients until you have a shaggy, rough dough. Cover the bowl with a clean shower cap or your choice of cover and leave the bowl on the counter for 1 hour.

Step 2: After an hour or so, perform the first set of pulls and folds until the dough feels less sticky and comes together into a soft ball. Cover the bowl again and leave it on your counter.

Step 3: Over the next few hours, do three more sets of pulls and folds on the dough, covering the dough after each set. Perform the final set before going to bed.

Step 4: Leave the covered bowl on the counter overnight, typically 8 to 10 hours, at 64 to 68°F (18 to 20°C).

Step 5: In the morning, the dough will have grown to double, maybe almost triple in size.

Gently but firmly perform a final set of pulls and folds on the dough to pull it into a ball. The dough will be bouncy and have a satisfying resistance you will be able to feel. Use your fingers to ease a hole into the middle of the ball of dough, lift the doughnut of dough from the bowl and place it in the prepared Bundt pan, placing it over and tucking it round the upright in the middle of the pan and cover it with the same shower cap.

(continued)

Master Recipe Bundt Pan Loaf (Continued)

Allow the dough to proof again, letting it grow again until it is level with the edge of the pan. This may take 2 to 4 hours, depending on the temperature of your kitchen. The surface will become smooth and the dough will spread into the crevices of the pan.

Step 6: When ready to bake, place parchment paper, followed by a baking sheet, on the top of the Bundt pan, to serve as a lid. Decide whether you would like to bake in a preheated oven or from a cold start. To bake from a preheated oven, set the oven to 325°F (160°C) convection or 350°F (180°C) conventional.

If you preheated the oven, bake for 50 minutes. If baking from a cold start, set the oven to 325°F (160°C) convection or 350°F (180°C) conventional and bake for 55 minutes.

After the baking time, remove from the oven, line the baking sheet with the parchment paper and set it aside, then turn the loaf out of the Bundt pan (it may benefit from sitting for 2 to 3 minutes on the counter to loosen, or need a tap on the counter to tip it out); it will be quite pale. Place the loaf, base down, on the prepared baking sheet and bake it uncovered for a further 10 minutes to brown slightly; it will remain a paler baked loaf than others.

Step 7: Remove from the oven, remove from the baking sheet and allow the loaf to cool on a wire rack for at least an hour before slicing. The cut loaf will have lots of crispy crust and a soft interior.

Top Tip:

Try baking any of the full-sized doughs in this book in a Bundt pan, or any pan you may have in the cupboard, and see what you can create!

Master Recipe Pullman Loaf

Baking in a Pullman loaf pan creates a square, sharp-edged sandwich loaf. One of the beauties of using a pan like this is that the pan does the shaping for you. For this loaf, I use my master recipe with slightly less flour; this makes a silky, bouncy dough and gives the dough space inside the pan without squashing it into a tight crumb when it bakes.

Prep: Feed your starter to generate the 50 grams (¼ cup) of active starter needed for the recipe; see page 18 for full details. Use a Pullman loaf pan, external size 8½ x 5 x 4½ inches (21.5 x 12.5 x 11.5 cm).

Makes 1 standard loaf

50 g (¼ cup) active starter

350 g (1½ cups) water

450 g (3¾ cups) strong white bread flour (see Top Tips)

7 g (1 tsp) salt, or to taste

Rice flour, for dusting

Step 1: In the early evening, in a large mixing bowl, roughly mix together all the ingredients, except the rice flour, until you have a shaggy, sticky dough. Cover the bowl with a clean shower cap or your choice of cover and leave the bowl on the counter for 1 hour.

Step 2: After an hour or so, perform the first set of pulls and folds; the dough will be soft and stretchy and will come into a soft ball. Cover the bowl again and leave it on your counter.

Step 3: Over the next few hours, do three more sets of pulls and folds on the dough, covering the dough after each set. Each time you pull the dough into a ball, stop. The dough will be light and easy to handle and will start to lose its ball shape soon after handling; this is all normal and as it should be due to the nature of the dough. Perform the final set before going to bed.

Step 4: Leave the covered bowl on the counter overnight, typically 8 to 10 hours, at 64 to 68°F (18 to 20°C).

Step 5: In the morning, the dough will have grown to double, possibly almost triple in size. It will be a lively, bouncy dough, soft but structured, and fun to handle. Sprinkle rice flour inside the pan and across the base. Gently but firmly perform a final set of pulls and folds on the dough to pull it into a ball and pick it up. Sprinkle more rice flour over the dough as it sits in your hand. If your pan is nonstick, you will not require much rice flour at all.

Place the dough, smooth side down, into the pan and sprinkle extra rice flour down the sides and across the top of the dough. Cover the pan with the same shower cap and place on the counter to proof again until the dough is level with the top edges of the pan; this may take several hours depending on the temperature in your kitchen. The key is to watch the dough and allow it time to do this important step. As a guide, this can take anywhere from 4 to 6 hours in my kitchen.

Step 6: When you are ready to bake, decide whether you would like to bake in a preheated oven or from a cold start. If preheating, set the oven to 350°F (180°C) convection or 400°F (200°C) conventional.

If you preheated the oven, put the lid on the pan and bake for 45 minutes. If using a cold start, place the covered pan of dough in the oven, set the temperature as directed and set a timer for 50 minutes.

Step 7: Remove from the oven and the pan, tap the base of the loaf and if it sounds hollow, the loaf is baked. If not, return it to the oven, out of the pan, directly onto the rack to bake for a

further 5 to 10 minutes. Remove from the oven and allow to cool on a wire rack for at least an hour before slicing.

Top Tips:

For a denser loaf, use 500 grams (4 cups) of flour; for a lighter loaf, use 400 grams (3½ cups) of flour. No other changes need to be made for either option.

Once you have made this recipe using strong white bread flour, it is a great recipe to make using other flours. I especially like it made with white spelt flour.

Ends of Bags Master Loaf

As we experiment with different flours, it is easy to end up with various bags with small amounts of leftover flours. This loaf includes a few leftover flours from my cupboard and the aim is to show you how you can use up your ends of bags. Get as creative as you would like by replacing the spelt, einkorn and rye flours with your own selection of leftover flours.

Prep: Feed your starter to generate the 50 grams (¼ cup) of active starter needed for the recipe; see page 18 for full details. Prepare an 11-inch (28-cm)-long oval banneton with rice flour and set aside a baking pan at least 12 inches (30 cm) long with a lid, plus parchment paper.

Makes 1 standard loaf

50 g (¼ cup) active starter

350 g (1½ cups) water

400 g (3 cups) strong white bread flour

25 g (¼ cup) whole-grain spelt flour

50 g (½ cup) whole-grain einkorn flour

25 g (¼ cup) light rye flour

7 g (1 tsp) salt, or to taste

Rice flour, for dusting

Step 1: In the early evening, in a large mixing bowl, roughly mix together all the ingredients, except the rice flour, until you have a shaggy, rough dough. It may feel quite stiff, but it will "give" as it rests. Cover the bowl with a clean shower cap or your choice of cover and leave the bowl on the counter for 1 hour.

Step 2: After an hour or so, perform the first set of pulls and folds; the dough will feel less stiff and you will be able to stretch the dough and bring it into a soft ball. Cover the bowl again and leave it on your counter.

Step 3: Over the next few hours, do three more sets of pulls and folds on the dough, stopping each time it comes into an easy ball, covering the dough after each set. Perform the final set before going to bed.

Step 4: Leave the covered bowl on the counter overnight, typically 8 to 10 hours, at 64 to 68°F (18 to 20°C).

Step 5: In the morning, the dough will have grown to double, almost triple in size, with a smooth surface. Sprinkle an extra layer of rice flour into the banneton. To place the dough in an oval banneton, lift and pull the dough over itself along one side of the bowl; this will be a heavy dough, slightly sticky from the flours. Turn the bowl around completely to the other side and pull the dough on that side again in a line to create a fat sausage of dough. Place the dough, smooth side down, in the banneton, sprinkling extra rice flour down the sides and across the top of the dough, cover it again with the same shower cap and place it in the fridge for at least 3 hours, up to 24.

Step 6: When you are ready to bake, decide whether you would like to bake in a preheated oven or from a cold start. If preheating, set the oven to 425°F (220°C) convection or 450°F (230°C) conventional.

Remove the cover from the banneton, then place the paper over the top of the banneton and the pan upside down over the top of them both. With one hand under the banneton and one on the pan, turn it all over together to turn the dough out of the banneton and into the pan. Score the dough.

If you preheated the oven, put the lid on the pan and bake for 50 minutes. If using a cold start, place the covered pan of dough in the oven, set the temperature as directed and set a timer for 55 minutes.

After the baking time, remove the pan from the oven. Open the lid and check the loaf. If you feel that it is looking pale, place the pan with the loaf back in the hot oven, minus the lid, for 5 to 10 minutes to brown the loaf to the color of your choice.

Step 7: Once baked, carefully remove the loaf from the pan, saving the parchment paper for next time, and allow the baked loaf to cool on a wire rack for at least an hour before slicing.

THE ENRICHED
Sourdough Collection

This collection of recipes is based on My Master Enriched Sourdough recipe (page 91), which can be described as a marriage of sourdough and brioche, with the beauty that it is made without the need for a mixer or huge arm muscles to work in the butter! The main recipes offer a slightly richer and a slightly lighter version, both of which bake to light, soft loaves. You will find doughs made with and without added flavors and ingredients, baked into different shapes, in different pans, and each and every one packed with taste.

My Master Enriched Sourdough recipe also provides a perfect vehicle for many flavors and shapes. I have provided some ideas here, but the possibilities are endless.

My Master Enriched Sourdough

This recipe takes the long, slow proof so wonderfully indicative of making sourdough, and it results in a light loaf with the hint of richness and sweetness of brioche. It produces a soft loaf with a close crumb perfect for sandwiches, or for lashings of butter on a toasted slice. The aroma as it toasts is glorious in itself!

PREP: Feed your starter to generate the 50 grams (¼ cup) of active starter needed for the recipe; see page 18 for full details. Line a 2-pound (900-g) loaf pan (9 x 5 inches [23 x 14 cm]) or an 8-inch (20-cm) round pan with a liner or parchment paper.

Makes 1 standard loaf

50 g (¼ cup) active starter

270 g (1 cup plus 1 tbsp) milk, cold or at room temperature (I use reduced-fat or 2% milk, but you can also use full-fat or whole milk)

1 large egg

1 large egg yolk (reserve egg white for brushing)

75 g (⅜ cup) butter (I use slightly salted butter), at room temperature

50 g (¼ cup) runny honey

500 g (4 cups) strong white bread flour

7 g (1 tsp) salt, or to taste

Step 1: In the early evening, in a large mixing bowl, roughly mix together all the ingredients, except the reserved egg white. It will be a very sticky dough, and it may be easier to use a bowl scraper or spatula to mix it at this stage. The butter will not be fully mixed through yet; it will become mixed in fully as you complete the next steps. Cover the bowl with a clean shower cap or your choice of cover and leave the bowl on the counter.

Step 2: After an hour, perform the first set of pulls and folds on the dough, lifting and pulling the dough across the bowl until it starts to come into a soft ball, then stop. The butter will still not be fully mixed in yet, but will become more so as you work with the dough. During this first set of pulls and folds, the dough will still be sticky, but keep working with it.

Cover the bowl again and leave it to sit on the counter.

Step 3: Over the next few hours, perform three more sets of pulls and folds on the dough, covering the bowl after each set. The dough will remain sticky but nicely stretchy and will come together into a nice soft ball each time. Do the final set before going to bed.

Step 4: Leave the covered bowl on the counter overnight, typically 8 to 12 hours, at 64 to 68°F (18 to 20°C).

Step 5: In the morning, hopefully the dough will have grown to triple in size, with a smooth surface. If the dough has not tripled yet, allow it a few more hours to continue to proof. This is a heavy dough and may take longer than a standard water-based dough to fully proof.

(continued)

Have your pan ready and place the flattened paper liner on the counter. To place the dough into the pan, repeat the same pulling and folding actions that you used to build the dough and gently lift and fold small handfuls of dough from one side of the bowl into the middle in a line. Turn the bowl 180 degrees and do the same on the other side so that you have a thick sausage of dough in the middle of the bowl.

Place your whole hand over the dough, turn the bowl upside down and gently ease the dough from the bowl into your hand. This will be a firm dough that does not take much handling to pull together. Place the dough, seam side down, on the paper and slip your hand out from underneath the dough. Use the paper to lift the dough into the pan, cover it with the same shower cap and leave it on the counter.

Allow the dough to proof again, letting it grow level with the edge of the pan and just peek over the top. This may take 2 to 6 hours, depending on the temperature of your kitchen. The surface will become smooth and the dough will spread to fill the pan.

Step 6: Mix the reserved egg white with a tablespoon (15 ml) of water and brush the top of the dough gently with it.

Step 7: When you are ready to bake, decide whether you would like to bake in a preheated oven or from a cold start. If preheating, set the oven to 325°F (160°C) convection or 350°F (180°C) conventional.

If you preheated the oven, bake uncovered for 40 minutes. If using a cold start, place the uncovered pan of dough in the oven, set the temperature as directed and set a timer for 45 minutes.

Step 8: Remove the loaf from the oven and the pan, remove the paper, tap the base of the loaf and if it sounds hollow, the loaf is baked. If not, return it to the oven, out of the pan, directly onto the rack to bake for a further 5 to 10 minutes. Remove from the oven and allow to cool on a wire rack.

My Enriched Sourdough Pesto Babka

Babkas are so much fun to make and my enriched dough is perfect for shaping and handling. For this babka, I have added pesto for a mix of sweet and savory, but the same recipe and process can be used for any sweet filling of your choice, too. I have used My Lighter Enriched Sourdough (page 96) for this loaf, but you could also use the richer version, My Master Enriched Sourdough (page 91).

PREP: Feed your starter to generate the 50 grams (¼ cup) of active starter needed for the recipe; see page 18 for full details. Line a 2-pound (900-g) loaf pan (9 x 5 inches [23 x 14 cm]) with a liner or parchment paper.

Makes 1 standard loaf

50 g (¼ cup) active starter

330 g (1¼ cups) reduced-fat or 2% milk

1 large egg yolk (reserve egg white for brushing)

50 g (¼ cup) butter (I use slightly salted butter), at room temperature

50 g (¼ cup) runny honey

500 g (4 cups) strong white bread flour, plus more for dusting

7 g (1 tsp) salt, or to taste

150 g (½ cup) basil pesto or pesto of your choice (see Top Tip)

Step 1: In the early evening, in a large mixing bowl, roughly mix together all the ingredients, except the reserved egg white and the pesto. It will be a very sticky dough, and it may be easier to use a bowl scraper or spatula to mix it at this stage. The butter will not be fully mixed through yet; it will become mixed in fully as you complete the next steps. Cover the bowl with a clean shower cap or your choice of cover and leave the bowl on the counter.

Step 2: After an hour, perform the first set of pulls and folds on the dough, lifting and pulling the dough across the bowl until it starts to come into a soft ball, then stop. The butter still may not be fully mixed in yet, but will become more so as you work with the dough. Cover the bowl again and leave it to sit on the counter.

During this first set of pulls and folds the dough will still be sticky but keep working with it.

Step 3: Over the next few hours, perform three more sets of pulls and folds on the dough, covering the bowl after each set. The dough will remain sticky but nicely stretchy and will come together into a nice soft ball each time. Do the final set before going to bed.

Step 4: Leave the covered bowl on the counter overnight, typically 8 to 12 hours, at 64 to 68°F (18 to 20°C).

Step 5: In the morning, hopefully the dough will have grown to triple in size, with a smooth surface. If the dough has not tripled yet, allow it a few more hours to continue to proof. This is a heavy dough and may take longer than a standard water-based dough to fully proof.

(continued)

My Enriched Sourdough Pesto Babka (Continued)

Once fully doubled in size, turn the dough out onto a floured surface, have your pan ready and place the flattened paper liner on the counter.

Pull and stretch the dough into an 8 x 15¾–inch (20 x 40–cm) rectangle. Spread the pesto evenly across the surface, right to the edges of the dough. Firmly roll the dough from one short side to the other into a sausage. Once rolled, use a dough knife or sharp knife to cut the sausage lengthwise down the middle into two equal pieces. Twist the two pieces together, then lift the whole dough onto your paper liner and use the paper to lift it into your pan. (For step-by-step photos of the twisted babka process, see the apricot babka recipe on page 135.)

Cover and allow the dough to proof again, letting it grow level with the edge of the pan. This may take 2 to 4 hours, depending on the temperature of your kitchen. The surface will become smooth and the dough will spread to fill the pan.

Step 6: Mix the egg white with a tablespoon (15 ml) of water and brush the top of the dough gently with it.

Step 7: When you are ready to bake, decide whether you would like to bake in a preheated oven or from a cold start. If preheating, set the oven to 325°F (160°C) convection or 350°F (180°C) conventional.

If you preheated the oven, bake uncovered for 45 minutes. If using a cold start, place the uncovered pan of dough in the oven, set the temperature as directed and set a timer for 50 minutes.

Step 8: Remove the loaf from the oven and the pan, remove the paper, tap the base of the loaf and if it sounds hollow, the loaf is baked. If not, return it to the oven, out of the pan, directly onto the rack to bake for a further 5 to 10 minutes. Remove from the oven and allow to cool on a wire rack.

Top Tip:

Replace the pesto with a sauce or paste of your choice, sweet or savory.

My Lighter Enriched Sourdough

This is a slightly lightened-up version of My Master Enriched Sourdough recipe (page 91), using less butter and egg. You could also lighten it even more, if you wish, by using a lower-fat milk. This recipe provides a perfect base for adding extras of your choice to, or for shaping and experimenting with. If the dough feels too soft and sticky to shape after the overnight or bulk proof, place the dough in its bowl in the fridge for 30 to 60 minutes to firm up, then use it and shape it directly from the fridge.

PREP: Feed your starter to generate the 50 grams (¼ cup) of active starter needed for the recipe; see page 18 for full details. Line an 8-inch (20-cm) round pan with a liner or parchment paper.

Makes 1 standard loaf

50 g (¼ cup) active starter

330 g (1¼ cups) reduced-fat or 2% milk or plant-based milk

1 large egg yolk (reserve egg white for brushing)

50 g (¼ cup) butter (I use slightly salted butter), at room temperature

50 g (¼ cup) runny honey

500 g (4 cups) strong white bread flour, plus more for dusting

7 g (1 tsp) salt, or to taste

Step 1: In the early evening, in a large mixing bowl, roughly mix together all the ingredients, except the reserved egg white. It will be a very sticky dough, and it may be easier to use a bowl scraper or spatula to mix it at this stage. Leave it roughly mixed, cover the bowl with a clean shower cap or your choice of cover and leave the bowl on the counter.

Step 2: After an hour, perform the first set of pulls and folds on the dough. Lift and pull the dough across the bowl until it starts to come into a soft ball, then stop; it will be a sticky dough, but will eventually easily come into a smooth soft ball. Cover the bowl again and leave it to sit on the counter.

Step 3: Over the next few hours, perform three more sets of pulls and folds on the dough, covering the bowl after each set. The dough will remain sticky but nicely stretchy and will come together into a nice soft ball each time. Do the final set before going to bed.

Step 4: Leave the covered bowl on the counter overnight, typically 8 to 12 hours, at 64 to 68°F (18 to 20°C).

Step 5: In the morning, hopefully the dough will have grown to triple in size, with a smooth surface. If the dough has not tripled yet, allow it a few more hours to continue to proof. This is a heavy dough and may take longer than a standard water-based dough to fully proof.

Once ready to shape, turn the dough out onto a floured surface. Have your pan ready and place the flattened paper liner on the counter. Cut the dough into seven equal pieces. Shape each portion into a smooth ball, and place the seven dough balls snugly in the paper liner inside your pan. Cover it with the same shower cap and leave it on the counter.

Allow the dough to proof again, letting it grow level with the edge of the pan and just peek over the top. This may take 2 to 6 hours, depending on the temperature of your kitchen. The surface will become smooth and the dough will spread to fill the pan.

Step 6: Mix the egg white with a tablespoon (15 ml) of water and brush the top of the dough gently with it.

Step 7: When you are ready to bake, decide whether you would like to bake in a preheated oven or from a cold start. If preheating, set the oven to 325°F (160°C) convection or 350°F (180°C) conventional.

If you preheated the oven, bake uncovered for 40 minutes. If using a cold start, place the uncovered pan of dough in the oven, set the temperature as directed and set a timer for 45 minutes.

Step 8: Remove the loaf from the oven and the pan, remove the paper, tap the base of the loaf and if it sounds hollow, the loaf is baked. If not, return it to the oven, out of the pan, directly onto the rack to bake for a further 5 to 10 minutes. Remove from the oven and allow to cool on a wire rack.

My Enriched Sourdough Jam-Filled Rolls

The mixture of jam and sourdough creates an almost doughnutlike experience, especially when eaten warm—be warned, these are seriously more-ish! Use your favorite flavor of jam; even add some fresh pieces of fruit, too, for more texture. I have used My Master Enriched Sourdough (page 91) for this loaf, but you could also use My Lighter Enriched Sourdough (page 96).

PREP: Feed your starter to generate the 50 grams (¼ cup) of active starter needed for the recipe; see page 18 for full details. Either line a large baking or cookie sheet with parchment paper and sprinkled with rice flour, or prepare fluted baby brioche pans (3⅛ inches [8 cm] in diameter and 1¼ inches [3 cm] deep), lined up ready to fill on a baking sheet.

Makes 16 snack-sized buns

50 g (¼ cup) active starter

270 g (1 cup plus 1 tbsp) milk, cold or room temperature (I use reduced-fat or 2% milk, but you can also use full-fat or whole milk)

1 large egg

1 large egg yolk (reserve egg white for brushing)

75 g (⅜ cup) butter (I use slightly salted butter), at room temperature

50 g (¼ cup) runny honey

500 g (4 cups) strong white bread flour, plus more for dusting

7 g (1 tsp) salt, or to taste

200 g (16 heaping [to double] teaspoons) jam of your choice

Powdered sugar, for sprinkling (optional)

Step 1: In the early evening, in a large mixing bowl, roughly mix together all the ingredients, except the reserved egg white and jam. It will be a very sticky dough, and it may be easier to use a bowl scraper or spatula to mix it at this stage. Leave it roughly mixed, cover the bowl with a clean shower cap or your choice of cover and leave the bowl on the counter.

Step 2: After an hour, perform the first set of pulls and folds on the dough, lifting and pulling the dough across the bowl until it starts to come into a soft ball, then stop. The butter will not be fully mixed in yet; it will become more so as you work with the dough. Cover the bowl again and leave it to sit on the counter.

During this first set of pulls and folds, the dough will still be sticky, but keep working with it.

Step 3: Over the next few hours, perform three more sets of pulls and folds on the dough, covering the bowl after each set. The dough will remain sticky but nicely stretchy and will come together into a nice soft ball each time. Do the final set before going to bed.

Step 4: Leave the covered bowl on the counter overnight, typically 8 to 12 hours, at 64 to 68°F (18 to 20°C).

Step 5: In the morning, hopefully the dough will have grown to triple in size, with a smooth surface. If the dough has not tripled yet, allow it a few more hours to continue to proof. This is a heavy dough and may take longer than a standard water-based dough to fully proof.

Once the dough has doubled, turn the dough out onto a lightly floured surface and pull the dough into a 14-inch (35-cm) square that is an even thickness all over. Using a dough knife or pizza cutter, cut the dough into sixteen equal squares.

Place a heaping teaspoon of jam in the middle of each square, pull the corners and edges of each square together and stick them together. Turn each parcel over and shape into a ball. Place each ball onto your prepared pan, allowing space between them to grow, or place them in your baby brioche pans.

Cover the balls with a large plastic bag and leave on the counter for the rolls to proof again for 2 to 3 hours, or until doubled in size.

Step 6: Mix the egg white with a tablespoon (15 ml) of water and brush the top of each ball gently with it.

Step 7: When you are ready to bake, decide whether you would like to bake in a preheated oven or from a cold start. If preheating, set the oven to 325°F (160°C) convection or 350°F (180°C) conventional.

If you preheated the oven, bake uncovered for 20 to 25 minutes. If using a cold start, place the uncovered pan(s) of dough in the oven, set the temperature as directed and set a timer for 25 to 30 minutes, or until nicely browned.

Step 8: Remove from the oven and place the rolls directly on a rack to cool briefly. These are best eaten warm, with an optional sprinkle of powdered sugar.

Top Tip:

This dough is sticky and ideal to use to make shapes for bakes; squeeze the edges of the dough together well to keep the jam encased.

Cinnamon and Raisin Enriched Bundt Pan Bake

I love using Bundt pans for my sourdough recipes; you can create such unusually shaped breads, whether sweet or savory, and create attractive showpieces for your dinner table. This creation includes cinnamon and raisins. Eat it on its own or slathered with butter! I have used My Master Enriched Sourdough (page 91) for this loaf, but you could also use My Lighter Enriched Sourdough (page 96).

PREP: Feed your starter to generate the 100 grams (½ cup) of active starter needed for the recipe; see page 18 for full details. You will need a 12-cup (2.8-L) Bundt pan, 10½ inches (26.7 cm) in diameter and 4½ inches (11.5 cm) deep.

Makes 1 Bundt loaf

100 g (½ cup) active starter

245 g (1 cup) milk, cold or at room temperature (I use reduced-fat or 2% milk, but you can also use full-fat or whole milk)

1 large egg

1 large egg yolk (reserve egg white for brushing)

75 g (⅜ cup) butter (I use slightly salted butter), at room temperature

50 g (¼ cup) runny honey

500 g (4 cups) strong white bread flour

8 g (1 tbsp) ground cinnamon

100 g (½ cup) raisins

7 g (1 tsp) salt, or to taste

Rice flour, for dusting

Step 1: In the early evening, in a large mixing bowl roughly mix together all the ingredients, except the reserved egg white and rice flour. It will be a sticky dough, and it may be easier to use a bowl scraper or spatula to mix it at this stage. The butter will not be fully mixed through yet; it will become mixed in fully as you complete the next steps. Cover the bowl with a clean shower cap or your choice of cover and leave the bowl on the counter.

Step 2: After an hour, perform the first set of pulls and folds on the dough, lifting and pulling the dough across the bowl until it starts to come into a soft ball, then stop. During this first set of pulls and folds the dough will still be sticky but keep working with it. The butter will still not be fully mixed in yet; it will become more so as you work with the dough. Cover the bowl again and leave it to sit on the counter.

Step 3: Over the next few hours, perform three more sets of pulls and folds on the dough, covering the bowl after each set. The dough will remain sticky but nicely stretchy and will come together into a nice soft ball each time, and the aroma should be wonderful. Do the final set before going to bed.

Step 4: Leave the covered bowl on the counter overnight, typically 8 to 12 hours, at 64 to 68°F (18 to 20°C).

Step 5: In the morning, hopefully the dough will have grown to double in size. If the dough has not doubled yet, allow it a few more hours to continue to proof. This is a heavy dough and may take longer than a standard water-based dough to fully proof.

Have ready your Bundt pan and rice flour in a shaker.

Once the dough is two to three times its original size, gently but firmly perform a final set of pulls and folds on the dough to pull it into a ball. Lift the ball of dough in your hand, and using rice flour, sprinkle some all over the dough. Using your fingers, ease a hole into the middle of the dough, like a huge bagel.

Place the dough into the Bundt pan, smooth side down, with the hole over the upright in the middle of the pan. Sprinkle extra rice flour around the edges, down the sides and inside of the dough. Cover the pan with the same cover.

Allow the dough to proof again, letting it grow to 1 to 1½ inches (2.5 to 4 cm) lower than the edge of the pan. This may take 2 to 4 hours, depending on the temperature of your kitchen. The surface will become smooth and the dough will spread into the pan.

Step 6: When you are ready to bake, decide whether you would like to bake in a preheated oven or from a cold start. Place parchment paper, followed by a baking sheet, on the top of the Bundt pan, to serve as a lid. If preheating, set the oven to 325°F (160°C) convection or 350°F (180°C) conventional.

If you preheated the oven, bake, covered, for 50 to 55 minutes. If using a cold start, place the covered pan of dough in the oven, set the temperature as directed and set a timer for 55 to 60 minutes, or until nicely browned.

Step 7: Remove the loaf from the oven, remove the baking sheet and paper, allow the loaf to cool for 5 minutes, then turn it out onto a wire rack to cool.

THE SPICED
Sourdough Collection

One of my great loves is cooking with spices. All the recipes in this section include spices, not only bringing together my food joys, but also different flavors and colors to the baked creations. My Breakfast Mix Master Loaf (page 105) embraces a chai-inspired blend. The Turmeric and Onion Seed Sandwich Loaf (page 112) brings a beautiful sunshine color to your plate. And the Smoked Paprika, Rosemary and Sun-Dried Tomato Master Loaf (page 110) brings a pizza infusion to your sourdough.

By allowing the loaves and rolls time to cool completely, the flavors of the spices will have time to develop and you will be able to taste them more than in warm loaves. If you also try toasted slices, the flavors shine through even more.

Once you have tried my creations, I hope you feel inspired to experiment with your own favorite spices using my quantities and processes.

My Breakfast Mix Master Loaf

I like to make my own porridge mix with oats, seeds and spices, and this loaf was created when I decided to add some of this breakfast mix to a dough mix to see what would happen. It was an immediate winner in my house, so it became the inspiration for this loaf. The spices add flavor and color, the seeds add a crunch and the oats add a wholesome finish to the loaf. One of the joys of this loaf is that the spices develop more flavor as the loaf cools, and even more so when the slices are toasted.

NOTES: Cinnamon can slow down proofing in bread doughs, hence this dough uses more starter than others to combat the effects of the cinnamon. I have provided the spices in spoon measurements only; the actual weights are so tiny, they may be difficult for you to weigh, and precision is not as essential for these. I use a combination of toasted pumpkin seeds, sunflower seeds and flaxseeds—you can use a mixture or single seed of your choice.

PREP: Feed your starter to generate the 100 grams (½ cup) of active starter needed for the recipe; see page 18 for full details. Prepare a round banneton, 8¾ inches (22 cm) in diameter and 3¼ inches (8.5 cm) deep, or a similarly sized bowl, with rice flour and set aside a large baking pan with a lid, plus parchment paper.

Makes 1 standard loaf

Dough

100 g (½ cup) active starter

325 g (1¼ cups) water

400 g (3 cups) strong white bread flour

50 g (¼ cup) steel-cut oats

50 g (¼ cup) mixed toasted seeds (see headnote)

7 g (1 tsp) salt, or to taste

Spices (see Top Tips)

1 tsp ground cinnamon

1 tsp ground turmeric

1 tsp ground ginger

¼ tsp ground nutmeg

¼ tsp ground cardamom

Small pinch of ground cloves

Step 1: In the early evening, in a large mixing bowl, roughly mix together all the ingredients until you have a shaggy, rough dough; it will be sticky and streaked with yellow from the turmeric. Cover the bowl with a clean shower cap or your choice of cover and leave the bowl on the counter for 1 hour.

Step 2: After an hour or so, perform the first set of pulls and folds; it will be stretchy and aromatic, fully yellow. Continue until it comes together into a soft ball. Cover the bowl again and leave it on your counter.

Step 3: Over the next few hours, do three more sets of pulls and folds on the dough, stopping each time it comes into a soft ball, covering the dough after each set. Perform the final set before going to bed.

Step 4: Leave the covered bowl on the counter overnight, typically 8 to 10 hours, at 64 to 68°F (18 to 20°C).

(continued)

My Breakfast Mix Master Loaf (Continued)

Step 5: In the morning, the dough will have grown to double in size.

Gently but firmly perform a final set of pulls and folds on the dough to pull it into a ball. The dough will be bouncy and have a satisfying resistance you will be able to feel. Place the dough, smooth side down, in the banneton, cover with the same shower cap and place in the fridge for at least 3 hours, up to 24 hours.

Step 6: When you are ready to bake, decide whether you would like to bake in a preheated oven or from a cold start. If preheating, set the oven to 425°F (220°C) convection or 450°F (230°C) conventional.

Remove the cover from the banneton, then place the paper over the top of the banneton and the pan upside down over the top of them both. With one hand under the banneton and one on the pan, turn it all over together to turn the dough out of the banneton and into the pan. Score the dome of dough.

If you preheated the oven, put the lid on the pan and bake for 50 minutes. If using a cold start, place the covered pan of dough in the oven, set the temperature as directed and set a timer for 55 minutes.

After the baking time for either option, remove the covered pan from the oven. Open the lid to check the loaf, and if you feel that your loaf is looking pale, place it back in the hot oven, in its pan, minus the lid, for 5 to 10 minutes, to brown the loaf to the color of your choice.

Step 7: Once baked, carefully remove the loaf from the pan, saving the parchment paper for next time, and allow the baked loaf to cool on a wire rack for at least an hour before slicing.

Top Tips:

Try some slices toasted; they release a wonderful aroma as they toast. If you would prefer not to buy all the individual spices, use 1 tablespoon (6 g) of a chai spice or an apple pie spice blend, plus 1 teaspoon of ground turmeric.

You may want to mix this dough initially with a bowl scraper and wear biodegradable gloves to protect your hands when handling it to prevent the turmeric from staining your hands.

Oat-Crusted Baby Breakfast Master Loaf

This is a baby version of My Breakfast Mix Master Loaf (page 105), full of seeds and spices, and with the oats creating a toasted crust instead of adding the oats to the dough as in the original version. The ingredients create an attractive, aromatic loaf full of flavor and the goodness from the seeds and spices, with the addition of the toasted oat crust.

NOTES: Cinnamon can slow down proofing in bread doughs, hence this dough uses more starter than others to combat the effects of the cinnamon. I have provided the spices in spoon measurements only; the actual weights are so tiny, they may be difficult for you to weigh, and precision is not as essential for these. I use a combination of toasted pumpkin seeds, sunflower seeds and flaxseeds—you can use a mixture or single seed of your choice.

PREP: Feed your starter to generate the 60 grams (¼ cup) of active starter needed for the recipe; see page 18 for full details. Prepare a round banneton, 6¾ inches (17 cm) in diameter and 3¼ inches (8.5 cm) deep, or a similarly sized bowl, with rice flour and set aside a large baking pan with a lid, plus parchment paper.

Makes 1 small loaf

Dough

60 g (¼ cup) active starter

200 g (scant 1 cup) water

300 g (2½ cups) strong white bread flour

30 g (¼ cup) mixed toasted seeds (see headnote)

3 g (½ tsp) salt, or to taste

Spices (see Top Tips)

½ tsp ground cinnamon

½ tsp ground turmeric

½ tsp ground ginger

Small pinch of ground nutmeg

Small pinch of ground cardamom

Very small pinch of ground cloves

50 g (½ cup) steel-cut oats, for crust

Step 1: In the early evening, in a large mixing bowl, roughly mix together all the ingredients, except the oats, until you have a shaggy, rough dough, with color starting to show through from the spices. Cover the bowl with a clean shower cap or your choice of cover and leave the bowl on the counter for 1 hour.

Step 2: After an hour or so, perform the first set of pulls and folds until the dough feels less sticky and comes together into a soft, fully yellow ball. Cover the bowl again and leave it on your counter.

Step 3: Over the next few hours, do three more sets of pulls and folds on the dough, covering the dough after each set. The dough will become stretchier with each handling. Perform the final set before going to bed.

Step 4: Leave the covered bowl on the counter overnight, typically 8 to 10 hours, at 64 to 68°F (18 to 20°C).

(continued)

Step 5: In the morning, you should be greeted by a bowl full of grown dough. Put the oats into a medium-sized bowl. Perform one last set of pulls and folds to form the dough into a nice ball. Lift the dough and place gently into the bowl of oats, smooth side down, then carefully roll it around to coat the smooth side in oats. Place the oat-covered dough in the banneton, oats side down. Sprinkle more oats down the sides and across the top. Cover the banneton with the same shower cap and place it in the fridge for 3 to 24 hours.

Step 6: When you are ready to bake, decide whether you would like to bake in a preheated oven or from a cold start. If preheating, set the oven to 425°F (220°C) convection or 450°F (230°C) conventional.

Remove the cover from the banneton, then place the paper over the top of the banneton and the pan upside down over the top of them both. With one hand under the banneton and one on the pan, turn it all over together to turn the dough out of the banneton and into the pan. Score the dome of dough, cutting through the oats.

If you preheated the oven, put the lid on and bake for 40 minutes. If using a cold start, place the covered pan of dough in the oven, set the temperature as directed and set a timer for 45 minutes.

After the baking time for either option, remove the covered pan from the oven. Open the lid to check the loaf; if you feel that the oat crust is looking pale, place it back in the hot oven, in its pan, minus the lid, for 5 to 10 minutes to brown the loaf to the color of your choice.

Step 7: Once baked, carefully remove the loaf from the pan, saving the parchment paper for next time, and allow the baked loaf to cool on a wire rack for at least an hour before slicing.

Top Tips:

If you would prefer not to buy all of the individual spices, use 1½ teaspoons (4 g) of a chai spice or an apple pie spice blend, plus ½ teaspoon of ground turmeric.

Follow the Baby Master Wedge Rolls (page 74) process from Step 5 to use this dough to make rolls.

You may want to mix this dough initially with a bowl scraper and wear biodegradable gloves to protect your hands when handling it to prevent the turmeric from staining your hands.

Smoked Paprika, Rosemary and Sun-Dried Tomato Master Loaf

The additions in this loaf give it an almost pizza-like flavor. The smoked paprika adds color as well as taste, the sun-dried tomatoes add bursts of moisture and sweetness and the olive oil adds a softness. For me, this loaf is wonderful to eat unadorned, but it also goes well with dips and oils, or topped with eggs.

NOTE: I use sun-dried tomatoes that are not heavily covered in oil. If yours are packed in oil, do not add the extra olive oil unless the dough feels dry. If your tomatoes are large slices, cut them into quarters before adding them to the dough.

PREP: Feed your starter to generate the 50 grams (¼ cup) of active starter needed for the recipe; see page 18 for full details. Prepare a round banneton, 8¾ inches (22 cm) in diameter and 3¼ inches (8.5 cm) deep, or a similarly sized bowl, with rice flour and set aside a large baking pan with a lid, plus parchment paper.

Makes 1 standard loaf

50 g (¼ cup) active starter

350 g (1½ cups) water

500 g (4 cups) strong white bread flour

100 g (½ cup) dry-packed sun-dried tomatoes (see Note and Top Tip)

30 g (⅛ cup) olive oil (see Note)

7 g (1 tbsp) smoked paprika

4 g (2 tsp) dried rosemary

7 g (1 tsp) salt, or to taste

Rice flour, for dusting

Step 1: In the early evening, in a large mixing bowl, roughly mix together all the ingredients, except the rice flour, until you have a shaggy, rough dough. Cover the bowl with a clean shower cap or your choice of cover and leave the bowl on the counter for 1 hour.

Step 2: After an hour or so, perform the first set of pulls and folds until the dough comes together into a soft ball that will already have a pink color. This will be a sticky dough. Cover the bowl again and leave it on your counter.

Step 3: Over the next few hours, do three more sets of pulls and folds on the dough, covering the dough after each set. The oil will make this a silky dough. Perform the final set before going to bed.

Step 4: Leave the covered bowl on the counter overnight, typically 8 to 10 hours, at 64 to 68°F (18 to 20°C).

Step 5: In the morning, hopefully the dough will have grown to double in size. Gently but firmly perform a final set of pulls and folds on the dough to pull it into a ball. Place the dough, smooth side down, in the banneton, sprinkling extra rice flour down the sides and across the top, cover with the same shower cap and place in the fridge for at least 3 hours, up to 24 hours.

Step 6: When you are ready to bake, decide whether you would like to bake in a preheated oven or from a cold start. If preheating, set the oven to 425°F (220°C) convection or 450°F (230°C) conventional.

Remove the cover from the banneton, then place the paper over the top of the banneton and the pan upside down over the top of them both. With one hand under the banneton and one on the pan, turn it all over together to turn the dough out of the banneton and into the pan. Score the dome of dough.

If you preheated the oven, put the lid on and bake for 50 minutes. If using a cold start, place the covered pan of dough in the oven, set the temperature as directed and set a timer for 55 minutes.

After the baking time for either option, remove the covered pan from the oven. Open the lid to check the loaf. Baking in a lidded pan produces a golden loaf. When you take the lid off, if you feel that your loaf is looking pale, place it back in the hot oven, in its pan, minus the lid, for 5 to 10 minutes to brown the loaf to the color of your choice.

Step 7: Once baked, carefully remove the loaf from the pan, saving the parchment paper for next time, and allow the baked loaf to cool on a wire rack for at least an hour before slicing.

Top Tip:

Replace part or all of the sun-dried tomatoes with halved olives.

Turmeric and Onion Seed Sandwich Loaf

The turmeric in this recipe produces such a bright yellow dough and loaf, it will bring a smile to your face. The onion seeds add a speckled effect as well as their subtle onion flavor. I have made this as a sandwich loaf, but the same dough can be used to make a round loaf.

PREP: Feed your starter to generate the 50 grams (¼ cup) of active starter needed for the recipe; see page 18 for full details. Line a 2-pound (900-g) loaf pan (9 x 5 inches [23 x 14 cm]) or an 8-inch (20-cm) round pan with a liner or parchment paper.

Makes 1 standard loaf

50 g (¼ cup) active starter

375 g (1¾ cups) water

500 g (4 cups) strong white bread flour

16 g (2 tbsp) onion seeds (see Top Tips)

2 g (2 tsp) ground turmeric

7 g (1 tsp) salt, or to taste

Step 1: In the early evening, in a large mixing bowl, roughly mix together all the ingredients until you have a ragged, rough, colored, speckled dough. Cover the bowl with a clean shower cap or your choice of cover and leave the bowl on the counter for 1 hour.

Step 2: After an hour or so, perform the first set of pulls and folds until the dough feels less sticky and comes together into a soft yellow and black speckled ball. Cover the bowl again and leave it on your counter.

Step 3: Over the next few hours, do three more sets of pulls and folds on the dough—it will be a stretchy dough—covering the dough after each set. Perform the final set before going to bed.

Step 4: Leave the covered bowl on the counter overnight, typically 8 to 10 hours, at 64 to 68°F (18 to 20°C).

Step 5: In the morning, the dough will have grown to double in size, with a smooth domed surface. Have your loaf pan ready and place the paper liner on the counter. Gently lift and fold small handfuls of dough from one side of the bowl into the middle in a line, using the same pulling and folding action as used previously. Turn the bowl 180 degrees and do the same on the other side so that you have a thick sausage of dough in the middle of the bowl.

With a wetted hand, place your whole hand over the dough, turn the bowl upside down and gently ease the dough from the bowl into your hand. Place the dough, seam side down, on the paper and slip your hand out from underneath the dough. Use the paper to lift the dough into the pan, cover it with the same shower cap and leave it on the counter.

Allow the dough to proof again, letting it grow level with the edge of the pan. This may take 2 to 3 hours, depending on the temperature of your kitchen. The surface will become smooth and the dough will spread to fill the pan.

Step 6: When you are ready to bake, decide whether you would like to bake in a preheated oven or from a cold start. If preheating, set the oven to 350°F (180°C) convection or 400°F (200°C) conventional.

If you preheated the oven, bake uncovered for 40 minutes. If using a cold start, place the uncovered pan of dough in the oven, set the temperature as directed and set a timer for 45 minutes.

Step 7: Remove the loaf from the oven and the pan, remove the paper, tap the base of the loaf and if it sounds hollow, the loaf is baked. If not, return it to the oven, out of the pan, directly onto the rack to bake for a further 5 to 10 minutes. Remove from the oven and allow to cool on a wire rack for at least an hour before slicing.

Top Tips:

If you cannot find onion seeds (Nigella sativa, also known as kalonji), use black sesame seeds for a similar look albeit a different flavor.

You may want to mix this dough initially with a bowl scraper and wear biodegradable gloves to protect your hands when handling it to prevent the turmeric from staining your hands.

THE SOFTER
Sourdough Collection

Sourdough can be a wonderfully crusty bread, but sometimes you, or someone you are baking for, might prefer a softer version. In this collection, you will find recipes for making your sourdough softer while still as tasty as always. The additions and amendments to these recipes can be applied to all the recipes in this book to create your own versions of each loaf.

By adding milk products to doughs, the baked loaves often bake darker than those made with water due to the fats from the dairy, have a less holey "crumb" and are soft inside and out, making them perfect for sandwiches, too. Using milk in sourdough also reduces the sourness of the loaf, so if you prefer a less sour flavor, this is a great way to produce that.

Half-Milk, Half-Water Baby Master Loaf

Replacing half of the water in the dough with milk will soften this baked loaf on the inside and outside. It will also produce a firm dough and a slightly tighter, less holey loaf, making it ideal for toast and sandwiches, as fillings do not drop through. Use any milk of your choice, either dairy or plant based. Nut milks and oat or coconut milk also produce slightly different flavors; I highly recommend trying variations.

PREP: Feed your starter to generate the 30 grams (⅛ cup) of active starter needed for the recipe; see page 18 for full details. Prepare a round banneton, 6¾ inches (17 cm) in diameter and 3¼ inches (8.5 cm) deep, or a similarly sized bowl, with rice flour, and set aside a large baking or cookie sheet, plus parchment paper.

Makes 1 small loaf

30 g (⅛ cup) active starter

110 g (½ cup) water

110 g (½ cup) milk, cold or at room temperature (I use reduced-fat or 2% milk, but you can also use full-fat or whole milk)

300 g (2½ cups) strong white bread flour

7 g (1 tsp) salt, or to taste

Rice flour, for dusting

Step 1: In a large mixing bowl, roughly mix together all the ingredients, except the rice flour, until you have a shaggy and rough, but stiff, dough. Cover the bowl with a clean shower cap or your choice of cover and leave the bowl on the counter for 1 hour.

Step 2: After an hour or so, perform the first set of pulls and folds until the dough comes together into a soft ball. This will be a much stiffer dough than those made with water, but also smoother. Cover the bowl again and leave it on your counter.

Step 3: Over the next few hours, do three more sets of pulls and folds on the dough, stopping each time it comes into a firm ball, covering the dough again after each set. Perform the final set before going to bed.

Step 4: Leave the covered bowl on the counter and allow the dough to grow until doubled in size, typically 8 to 10 hours, at 64 to 68°F (18 to 20°C). Doughs made with milk can often take longer than those made with water.

Step 5: Once fully proofed, the surface of the dough will be smooth and lightly domed upwards; firmly perform a final set of pulls and folds on the dough to pull it into a ball.

Place the dough, smooth side down, in the banneton, sprinkle extra rice flour down the sides and across the top, cover with the same shower cap and place in the fridge for at least 3 hours, maximum 24 hours.

Step 6: When you are ready to bake, decide whether you would like to bake in a preheated oven or from a cold start. If preheating, set the oven to 425°F (220°C) convection or 450°F (230°C) conventional.

Remove the cover from the banneton, then place the paper over the top of the banneton and the pan upside down over the top of them both. With one hand under the banneton and one on the pan, turn it all over together to turn the dough out of the banneton and into the pan. Score the dome of dough.

If you preheated the oven, put the lid on and bake for 40 minutes. If using a cold start, place the covered pan of dough in the oven, set the temperature as directed and set a timer for 45 minutes.

After the baking time for either option, remove the covered pan from the oven. Open the lid to check the loaf; if you feel that your loaf is looking paler than you would like, place it back in the hot oven, in its pan, minus the lid, for 5 to 10 minutes to brown the loaf to the color of your choice.

Step 7: Once baked, carefully remove the loaf from the pan, saving the parchment paper for next time, and allow the baked loaf to cool on a wire rack for at least an hour before slicing.

Whole-Grain Spelt and Milk Sandwich Loaf

This is a wholesome filling loaf packed with flavor. Adding milk, especially full-fat or whole milk, to the dough produces loaves with a softer crumb and crust than those made with water. Baking it as a sandwich loaf and including spelt flour in the dough add even more softness. In this loaf, I have used full-fat cow's milk; this can be replaced with the milk of your choice, including nondairy milk alternatives.

PREP: Feed your starter to generate the 50 grams (¼ cup) of active starter needed for the recipe; see page 18 for full details. Line a 2-pound (900-g) loaf pan (9 x 5 inches [23 x 14 cm]) or an 8-inch (20-cm) round pan with a liner or parchment paper.

Makes 1 standard loaf

50 g (¼ cup) active starter

400 g (2 cups) full-fat milk, cold or at room temperature (use reduced-fat or 2% milk for a lighter loaf)

250 g (2 cups) strong white bread flour

250 g (2¼ cups) whole-grain spelt flour (see Top Tip)

7 g (1 tsp) salt, or to taste

Step 1: In a large mixing bowl, roughly mix together all the ingredients until you have a shaggy, rough, sticky dough. Cover the bowl with a clean shower cap or your choice of cover and leave the bowl on the counter for 1 hour.

Step 2: After an hour or so, perform the first set of pulls and folds until the dough comes together into a smooth ball; this will be a stiff dough. Cover the bowl again and leave it on your counter.

Step 3: Over the next few hours, do three more sets of pulls and folds on the dough, stopping each time it comes into a ball and covering the dough again after each set. This will be a heavy, sticky dough. Perform the final set before going to bed.

Step 4: Leave the covered bowl on the counter and allow the dough to grow until doubled in size, typically 8 to 10 hours, at 64 to 68°F (18 to 20°C). Doughs made with milk can often take longer to fully proof than those made with water.

Step 5: In the morning, hopefully the dough will have grown to double in size, with a smooth, slightly domed surface. Have your loaf pan ready and place the paper liner on the counter. Gently lift and fold small handfuls of dough from one side of the bowl into the middle in a line, using the same pulling and folding action as used previously. Turn the bowl 180 degrees and do the same on the other side so that you have a thick sausage of dough in the middle of the bowl. This will be a heavy, sticky dough.

With a wetted hand, place your whole hand over the dough, turn the bowl upside down and gently ease the dough from the bowl into your hand. Place the dough, seam side down, on the paper and slip your hand out from underneath the dough. Use the paper to lift the dough into the pan, cover it with the same shower cap and leave it on the counter.

Allow the dough to proof again, letting it grow level with the edge of the pan and just peek over the top. This may take 2 to 3 hours, depending on the temperature of your kitchen. The surface will become smooth and the dough will spread to fill the pan.

Step 6: When you are ready to bake, decide whether you would like to bake in a preheated oven or from a cold start. If preheating, set the oven to 350°F (180°C) convection or 400°F (200°C) conventional.

If you preheated the oven, bake uncovered for 40 minutes. If using a cold start, place the uncovered pan of dough in the oven, set the temperature as directed and set a timer for 45 minutes.

Step 7: Remove the loaf from the oven and the pan, remove the paper, tap the base of the loaf and if it sounds hollow, the loaf is baked. If not, return it to the oven, out of the pan, directly onto the rack to bake for a further 5 to 10 minutes. Remove the loaf from the oven and allow it to cool on a wire rack for at least an hour before slicing.

Top Tip:

If you would like, you can replace the whole-grain spelt flour with white spelt flour or all-purpose flour.

Buttermilk and Spelt Loaf with Pine Nuts and Oats

For this recipe, I have revisited one of the most popular recipes from my previous book; the dough is made using buttermilk and white spelt flour. The natural dairy fats in the buttermilk and the lightness of the flour produce a soft, fluffy loaf. In this version, I have added pine nuts, which add a soft nuttiness without having a hard crunch, and an oat crust for an extra toasted flavor. However, this loaf is just as tasty without the pine nuts or oat crust.

PREP: Feed your starter to generate the 50 grams (¼ cup) of active starter needed for the recipe; see page 18 for full details. Prepare a banneton 8¾ inches (22 cm) in diameter and 3¼ inches (8.5 cm) deep, or a similarly sized bowl, with rice flour, and set aside a large, round baking pan with a lid.

Makes 1 standard loaf

50 g (¼ cup) active starter

300 g (1¼ cups) buttermilk, at room temperature or cold

100 g (scant ½ cup) water

500 g (4 cups) white spelt flour (see Top Tips)

30 g (⅛ cup) raw pine nuts

7 g (1 tsp) salt, or to taste

50 g (¼ cup) raw oats (thick-cut or steel-cut oats work perfectly)

Step 1: In a large mixing bowl, roughly mix together all the ingredients, except the oats, until you have a shaggy, rough dough; this will be a stiff mixture. Cover the bowl with a clean shower cap or your choice of cover and leave the bowl on the counter for 1 hour.

Step 2: After an hour or so, perform the first set of pulls and folds until the dough comes together into a soft ball. This will be a much stiffer dough than those made with water; you may need to turn the dough over onto itself rather than stretch it at this point. Cover the bowl again and leave it on your counter.

Step 3: Over the next few hours, do three more sets of pulls and folds on the dough, covering the dough after each set; the dough will remain firm but will become stretchier with each handling. Perform the final set before going to bed.

Step 4: Leave the covered bowl on the counter and allow the dough to grow until doubled in size, typically 8 to 10 hours, at 64 to 68°F (18 to 20°C). Doughs made with milk products can often take longer than those made with water.

(continued)

Buttermilk and Spelt Loaf with Pine Nuts and Oats (Continued)

Step 5: In the morning, the dough will have grown to double in size, with a smooth, slightly domed surface. Put the oats into a medium-size to large bowl. Perform one last set of pulls and folds to form the dough into a nice ball. Place your hand over the whole dough, turn the whole bowl over and let the dough fall into your hand. Place the dough gently into the bowl of oats, smooth side down, and carefully roll it around to coat the smooth side in oats. Place the oat-covered dough in the banneton, oat side down. Sprinkle more oats down the sides and across the top. Cover the banneton and place it in the fridge for 3 to 24 hours.

Step 6: After at least 3 hours, and when you are ready to bake, decide whether you would like to bake in a preheated oven or from a cold start. If preheating, set the oven to 425°F (220°C) convection or 450°F (230°C) conventional.

Remove the cover from the banneton, then place the paper over the top of the banneton and the pan upside down over the top of them both. With one hand under the banneton and one on the pan, turn it all over together to turn the dough out of the banneton and into the pan. Score the dome of dough, cutting through the softened oats as necessary.

If you preheated the oven, put the lid on the pan and bake for 50 minutes. If using a cold start, place the covered pan of dough in the oven, set the temperature as directed and set a timer for 55 minutes.

After the baking time for either option, remove the covered pan from the oven. Open the lid to check the loaf; if you would like more color on your loaf, place the pan back in the hot oven, minus the lid, for 5 to 10 minutes.

Step 7: Once baked, carefully remove the loaf from the pan, saving the parchment paper for next time, and allow the baked loaf to cool on a wire rack for at least an hour before slicing.

Top Tips:

If you do not have access to white spelt flour, replace it with all-purpose flour or whole-grain spelt flour.

Collect any toasted oats that fall off the loaf and add them to your morning breakfast.

Olive Oil and Herb Master Loaf

This is a marvelously savory loaf that can be eaten and enjoyed in so many ways, on its own or alongside various meal choices. Adding oils to doughs results in softer loaves. It can also keep your bread softer and fresher for longer than those without it. For this loaf, I have used olive oil and added herbs for an extra flavor. You can use any oil of your choice, and omit or change the herbs according to your preference.

PREP: Feed your starter to generate the 50 grams (¼ cup) of active starter needed for the recipe; see page 18 for full details. Prepare an 11-inch (28-cm)-long oval banneton with rice flour and set aside a baking pan, at least 12 inches (30 cm) long with a lid, plus parchment paper.

Makes 1 standard loaf

50 g (¼ cup) active starter

350 g (1½ cups) water

25 g (2 tbsp) olive oil

500 g (4 cups) strong white bread flour

1 g (2 tsp) dried basil

1 g (2 tsp) dried oregano

1 g (2 tsp) dried thyme

7 g (1 tsp) salt, or to taste

Rice flour, for dusting

Step 1: In a large mixing bowl, roughly mix together all the ingredients, except the rice flour, until you have a shaggy, rough dough. Cover the bowl with a clean shower cap or your choice of cover and leave the bowl on the counter for 1 hour.

Step 2: After an hour or so, perform the first set of pulls and folds until the dough comes together into a soft, silky ball; you will be able to feel the oil in the dough. Cover the bowl again and leave it on your counter.

Step 3: Over the next few hours, do three more sets of pulls and folds on the dough, stopping each time the dough comes into a soft ball and covering the dough again after each set. Perform the final set before going to bed.

Step 4: Leave the covered bowl on the counter and allow the dough to grow until doubled in size, typically 8 to 10 hours, at 64 to 68°F (18 to 20°C).

Step 5: In the morning, the dough will have grown to double, almost triple in size. Sprinkle an extra layer of rice flour into the banneton. To place the dough in an oval banneton, lift and pull the dough over itself along one side of the bowl. Turn the bowl around completely to the other side and pull the dough on that side again in a line to create a fat sausage of dough. This will be a wobbly soft dough, but fun to handle. Place the dough, smooth side down, in the banneton, sprinkling extra rice flour down the sides and across the top of the dough, cover it again with the same shower cap and place it in the fridge for at least 3 hours, maximum 24 hours.

(continued)

Olive Oil and Herb Master Loaf (Continued)

Step 6: After at least 3 hours, and when you are ready to bake, decide whether you would like to bake in a preheated oven or from a cold start. If preheating, set the oven to 425°F (220°C) convection or 450°F (230°C) conventional.

Remove the cover from the banneton, then place the paper over the top of the banneton and the pan upside down over the top of them both. With one hand under the banneton and one on the pan, turn it all over together to turn the dough out of the banneton and into the pan. Score the dough.

If you preheated the oven, put the lid on the pan and bake for 50 minutes. If using a cold start, place the covered pan of dough in the oven, set the temperature as directed and set a timer for 55 minutes.

After the baking time for either option, remove the covered pan from the oven. Open the lid to check the loaf, which will be a pale bake; if after 50 minutes you would like more color on your loaf, place the pan back in the hot oven, minus the lid, for 5 to 10 minutes.

Step 7: Once baked, carefully remove the loaf from the pan, saving the parchment paper for next time, and allow the baked loaf to cool on a wire rack for at least an hour before slicing. The smell will be tantalizing!

Top Tip:

Spread toasted slices with tomato sauce and cheese, then grill to create quick pizza slices.

Oat Milk Cranberry Loaf

Sourdough loves nondairy milks. The dough enjoys the added sugars from the milk and benefits from the extra flavor the various types of milk bring. I have used oat milk in this loaf, but you could also use coconut milk (either the coconut milk beverage that you find in cartons, or the thinner milk underneath the coconut cream in a can), soy milk or the nut milk of your choice. They all work with this recipe. I have also added dried cranberries for delicious bursts of tart sweetness, though you may prefer to leave them out or use a different dried fruit of your choice.

PREP: Feed your starter to generate the 50 grams (¼ cup) of active starter needed for the recipe; see page 18 for full details. Prepare a round banneton, 8¾ inches (22 cm) in diameter and 3¼ inches (8.5 cm) deep, or a similarly sized bowl, with rice flour and set aside a large baking pan with a lid, plus parchment paper.

Makes 1 standard loaf

---

50 g (¼ cup) active starter

375 g (1¾ cups) oat milk, cold or at room temperature

250 g (2 cups) strong white bread flour

250 g (2½ cups) white spelt flour (see Top Tip)

75 g (¾ cup) dried cranberries

7 g (1 tsp) salt, or to taste

Rice flour, for dusting

Step 1: In a large mixing bowl, roughly mix together all the ingredients, except the rice flour, until you have a shaggy, rough dough. Cover the bowl with a clean shower cap or your choice of cover and leave the bowl on the counter for 1 hour.

Step 2: After an hour or so, perform the first set of pulls and folds until the dough comes together into a soft ball. With the use of milk plus dried cranberries, this will be a much stiffer dough than those made with water. Cover the bowl again and leave it on your counter.

Step 3: Over the next few hours, do three more sets of pulls and folds on the dough, covering the dough after each set; it will become nicely stretchy and smooth. Perform the final set before going to bed.

Step 4: Leave the covered bowl on the counter and allow the dough to grow until doubled in size, typically 8 to 10 hours, at 64 to 68°F (18 to 20°C).

Step 5: Once fully proofed, the surface of the dough will be smooth and lightly domed upwards. Gently but firmly perform a final set of pulls and folds on the dough to pull it into a ball. The cranberries will be studded throughout the dough and you will already be able to smell them.

Place the dough, smooth side down, in the banneton, sprinkling extra rice flour down the sides and across the top of the dough, cover with the same shower cap and place in the fridge for at least 3 hours, maximum 24 hours.

Step 6: After at least 3 hours, and when you are ready to bake, decide whether you would like to bake in a preheated oven or from a cold start. If preheating, set the oven to 425°F (220°C) convection or 450°F (230°C) conventional.

Remove the cover from the banneton, then place the paper over the top of the banneton and the pan upside down over the top of them both. With one hand under the banneton and one on the pan, turn it all over together to turn the dough out of the banneton and into the pan. Score the dome of dough; the lame will cut through any cranberries near the surface. Push any cranberries on the surface into the dough to prevent any burning.

If you preheated the oven, put the lid on the pan and bake for 50 minutes. If using a cold start, place the covered pan of dough in the oven, set the temperature as directed and set a timer for 55 minutes.

After the baking time for either option, remove the covered pan from the oven. Open the lid to check the loaf; if you would like more color on your loaf, place the pan back in the hot oven, minus the lid, for 5 to 10 minutes.

Step 7: Once baked, carefully remove the loaf from the pan, saving the parchment paper for next time, and allow the baked loaf to cool on a wire rack for at least an hour before slicing.

Top Tip:

If you do not have access to white spelt flour, replace it with all-purpose flour or whole-grain spelt flour.

Milk Powder Poppy Seed Master Loaf

Adding milk powder when mixing up this dough brings a softness and sweetness to the baked loaf; if you use coconut milk powder as I have here, it produces an even softer loaf and is actually my preference between using a dairy or nondairy milk powder. I fully encourage you to try it both ways and see which is your favorite. Milk powder also makes this dough very practical if you do not have enough actual milk for other milk-based recipes.

PREP: Feed your starter to generate the 50 grams (¼ cup) of active starter needed for the recipe; see page 18 for full details. Prepare an 11-inch (28-cm)-long oval banneton with rice flour and set aside a baking pan, at least 12 inches (30 cm) long with a lid, plus parchment paper.

Makes 1 standard loaf

50 g (¼ cup) active starter

350 g (1½ cups) water

500 g (4 cups) strong white bread flour

25 g (¼ cup) poppy seeds

14 g (2 tbsp) coconut milk powder

7 g (1 tsp) salt, or to taste

Rice flour, for dusting

Step 1: In a large mixing bowl, roughly mix together all the ingredients, except the rice flour, until you have a shaggy, sticky, rough dough. Cover the bowl with a clean shower cap or your choice of cover and leave the bowl on the counter for 1 hour.

Step 2: After an hour or so, perform the first set of pulls and folds until the dough comes together into a soft ball. This dough will feel sticky from the milk powder and textured with the seeds. Cover the bowl again and leave it on your counter.

Step 3: Over the next few hours, do three more sets of pulls and folds on the dough, covering the dough after each set; it will become less sticky with each handling and nicely stretchy. Perform the final set before going to bed.

Step 4: Leave the covered bowl on the counter and allow the dough to grow until doubled in size, typically 8 to 10 hours, at 64 to 68°F (18 to 20°C).

Step 5: In the morning, the dough should have grown to double in size, with a smooth, bumpy surface and speckled with the poppy seeds. Sprinkle an extra layer of rice flour in the banneton. To place the dough into an oval banneton, lift and pull the dough over itself along one side of the bowl. Turn the bowl around completely to the other side and pull the dough on that side again in a line to create a fat sausage of dough. This will be a satisfyingly firm dough to handle. Place the dough, smooth side down, in the banneton, sprinkling extra rice flour down the sides and across the top of the dough, cover it again with the same shower cap and place it in the fridge for at least 3 hours, up to 24 hours.

Step 6: After at least 3 hours, and when you are ready to bake, decide whether you would like to bake in a preheated oven or from a cold start. If preheating, set the oven to 425°F (220°C) convection or 450°F (230°C) conventional.

Remove the cover from the banneton, then place the paper over the top of the banneton and the pan upside down over the top of them both. With one hand under the banneton and one on the pan, turn it all over together to turn the dough out of the banneton and into the pan. Score the dome of dough.

If you preheated the oven, put the lid on the pan and bake for 50 minutes. If using a cold start, place the covered pan of dough in the oven, set the temperature as directed and set a timer for 55 minutes.

After the baking time for either option, remove the covered pan from the oven. Open the lid to check the loaf; if you would like more color on your loaf, place the pan back in the hot oven, minus the lid, for 5 to 10 minutes.

Step 7: Once baked, carefully remove the loaf from the pan, saving the parchment paper for next time, and allow the baked loaf to cool on a wire rack for at least an hour before slicing.

THE FILLED
Collection

The loaves in this collection all have additional ingredients mixed into the dough, elevating our beloved sourdough to new heights of decadence. The recipes can be an introduction to adding your favorite things to your doughs, and can form a guide for where to start for any extras you would like to add. The world is literally your oyster.

The methods show how to add extra ingredients right from the beginning or later in the process; these demonstrate perfect ways for you to add your own extras.

Cheese, Fig and Walnut Sandwich Loaf

Melted cheese, bursts of sweet figs and the crunch of walnuts enhance this sourdough loaf, virtually making it a meal in a loaf. Spread on the butter and call it lunch or dinner in one go! I have made this by stretching out and filling the dough and baking it in a sandwich loaf pan; this way, the soft cheese does not break down too much before baking, so you get some good chunks of it in your slices. I have used blue cheese for its bold, rich flavor, but any similar soft cheese, such as Gorgonzola, goat cheese or even feta will work nicely.

PREP: Feed your starter to generate the 50 grams (¼ cup) of active starter needed for the recipe; see page 18 for full details. Line a 2-pound (900-g) loaf pan (9 x 5 inches [23 x 14 cm]) or an 8-inch (20-cm) round pan with a liner or parchment paper.

Makes 1 standard loaf

50 g (¼ cup) active starter

350 g (1½ cups) water

500 g (4 cups) strong white bread flour, plus more for dusting

7 g (1 tsp) salt, or to taste

Mix-Ins

75 g (½ cup) blue cheese (see headnote), cut into small pieces

50 g (½ cup) walnut pieces

100 g (Ð cup) chopped dried figs, stalks removed

Step 1: In the early evening, in a large mixing bowl, roughly mix together all the ingredients, except the cheese, walnuts and figs, until you have a shaggy, rough dough. Cover the bowl with a clean shower cap or your choice of cover and leave the bowl on the counter for 1 hour.

Step 2: After an hour or so, perform the first set of pulls and folds until the dough feels less sticky and comes together into a soft ball. Cover the bowl again and leave it on your counter.

Step 3: Over the next few hours, do three more sets of pulls and folds on the dough, covering the dough after each set. Perform the final set before going to bed.

Step 4: Leave the covered bowl on the counter overnight, typically 8 to 10 hours, at 64 to 68°F (18 to 20°C).

Step 5: In the morning, the dough will have grown to double in size; turn the dough out onto a floured surface, have your pan ready and place the flattened paper liner on the counter.

Pull and stretch the dough into a 7½ x 15¾–inch (19 x 40–cm) rectangle (see Top Tip). Sprinkle the cheese, walnuts and figs evenly across the surface. Firmly roll the dough from one short side to the other into a sausage.

With a wetted hand, place your whole hand over the dough, turn the bowl upside down and gently ease the dough from the bowl into your hand. Place the dough, seam side down, on the paper and slip your hand out

from underneath the dough. Use the paper to lift the dough into the pan, cover it with the same shower cap and leave it on the counter.

Allow the dough to proof again, letting it grow level with the edge of the pan and just peek over the top. This may take 2 to 3 hours, depending on the temperature of your kitchen. The surface will become smooth and the dough will spread to fill the pan.

Step 6: When you are ready to bake, decide whether you would like to bake in a preheated oven or from a cold start. If preheating, set the oven to 350°F (180°C) convection or 400°F (200°C) conventional.

If you preheated the oven, bake uncovered for 40 minutes. If using a cold start, place the uncovered pan of dough in the oven, set the temperature as directed and set a timer for 45 minutes.

Step 7: Remove the loaf from the oven and the pan, remove the paper, tap the base of the loaf and if it sounds hollow, the loaf is baked. If not, return it to the oven, out of the pan, directly onto the rack to bake for a further 5 to 10 minutes. Remove from the oven and allow to cool on a wire rack for at least an hour before slicing.

Top Tip:

When you stretch out the dough in Step 5, stretch out the width to match the length of the loaf pan you will be using to bake it in. It makes it easier to ensure it is the right size for the pan.

Apricot and Almond Babka Loaf

Babkas are so much fun to make and look so impressive before and after baking, and in and out of the pan, that I end up with multiple photos of every stage to be able to relive every part, not just the eating! By using a dough made with milk, the dough is firmer to handle than a standard water-based dough, which makes it easier to form.

PREP: Feed your starter to generate the 50 grams (¼ cup) of active starter needed for the recipe; see page 18 for full details. Line a 2-pound (900-g) loaf pan (9 x 5 inches [23 x 14 cm]) or an 8-inch (20-cm) round pan with a liner or parchment paper.

Makes 1 standard loaf

50 g (¼ cup) active starter

200 g (scant 1 cup) almond milk or any milk of your choice

150 g (⅔ cup) water

500 g (4 cups) strong white bread flour, plus more for dusting

7 g (1 tsp) salt, or to taste

Mix-Ing

150 g (½ cup) apricot jam or conserve (see Top Tips)

50 g (¼ cup) dried apricots, quartered (see Top Tips)

30 g (⅛ cup) flaked almonds

Step 1: In the early evening, in a large mixing bowl, roughly mix together all the ingredients except the jam, dried apricots and flaked almonds, until you have a shaggy, rough dough. Cover the bowl with a clean shower cap or your choice of cover and leave the bowl on the counter for 1 hour.

Step 2: After an hour or so, perform the first set of pulls and folds until the dough feels less sticky and comes together into a soft ball; it may be slightly stiff due to the milk in the dough. Cover the bowl again and leave it on your counter.

Step 3: Over the next few hours, do three more sets of pulls and folds on the dough; it will be nicely stretchy, covering the dough after each set. Perform the final set before going to bed.

Step 4: Leave the covered bowl on the counter overnight, typically 8 to 10 hours, at 64 to 68°F (18 to 20°C).

Step 5: In the morning, hopefully the dough will have grown to double in size. This is a heavier dough than those made with just water and may take longer than a standard water-based dough to fully proof, so if it needs longer, keep it covered and allow it to double in size.

Once fully doubled in size, turn the dough out onto a floured surface, have your pan ready and place the flattened paper liner on the counter.

(continued)

Apricot and Almond Babka Loaf (Continued)

Pull and stretch the dough into an 8 x 15¾–inch (20 x 40–cm) rectangle (see Top Tips). Spread the jam evenly across the dough, all the way to the edges, then sprinkle with the apricots and flaked almonds evenly across the surface. Firmly roll the dough from one short side to the other into a sausage.

Once rolled, use a dough knife or sharp knife to cut the sausage lengthwise down the middle into two equal pieces. Twist the two pieces together, then lift the whole dough onto your paper liner and use the paper to lift it into your pan.

Allow the dough to proof again, letting it grow level with the edge of the pan. This may take 2 to 4 hours, depending on the temperature of your kitchen. The surface will become smooth and the dough will spread to fill the pan.

Step 6: When you are ready to bake, decide whether you would like to bake in a preheated oven or from a cold start. If preheating, set the oven to 325°F (160°C) convection or 350°F (180°C) conventional.

If you preheated the oven, bake uncovered for 40 to 45 minutes. If using a cold start, place the uncovered pan of dough in the oven, set the temperature as directed and set a timer for 45 to 50 minutes.

Step 7: Remove the loaf from the oven and the pan, remove the paper, tap the base of the loaf and if it sounds hollow, the loaf is baked. If not, return it to the oven, out of the pan, directly onto the oven rack to bake for a further 5 to 10 minutes. Remove the loaf from the oven and allow it to cool on a wire rack for at least an hour before slicing.

Top Tips:

If your apricot conserve contains a good quantity of apricot pieces, use 200 grams (¾ cup) of conserve and no additional dried apricots.

In Step 5, stretch out the dough to match the length of your baking pan; it will make the dough easier to lift into the pan

After the main overnight proof, gather all of the ingredients ready to fill the loaf.

Turn the dough out onto a floured surface and have your lined loaf pan ready.

Stretch the dough into a rectangle and cover with jam, apricots and almonds.

Start to roll the dough from one of the short sides.

Roll it into a firm log; the dough will stick to itself to close the roll.

Using a nonstick dough knife or sharp knife, cut the roll in half lengthwise.

Twist the two pieces over themselves, then lift the dough onto the loaf pan liner.

Cover the pan and leave on the counter to proof again.

Once the dough has grown to fill the pan, bake as per the recipe.

Cheese and Onion Chutney Sandwich Loaf

A bread classic: cheese and chutney. Instead of eating them on top of freshly baked sourdough, add them into the dough to create a bread you'll keep going back to. I have used a portion of whole wheat flour in this dough to add extra flavor and texture; you could also use Khorasan flour or whole-grain spelt flour. The flour also adds a deeper flavor to the loaf that complements the strength of the cheese and chutney. My preference is always to use sharp Cheddar cheese, but this would also work wonderfully with Red Leicester, aged Comté or a strong Gouda.

PREP: Feed your starter to generate the 50 grams (¼ cup) of active starter needed for the recipe; see page 18 for full details. Line a 2-pound (900-g) loaf pan (9 x 5 inches [24 x 14 cm]) or an 8-inch (20-cm) round pan with a liner or parchment paper.

Makes 1 standard loaf

50 g (¼ cup) active starter

350 g (1½ cups) water

400 g (3¼ cups) strong white bread flour, plus more for dusting

100 g (¾ cup) whole wheat flour

7 g (1 tsp) salt, or to taste

Mix-Ins

150 g (1¼ cups) cubed Cheddar cheese or the cheese of your choice

100 g (Đ cup) store-bought or homemade red onion chutney

Step 1: In the early evening, in a large mixing bowl, roughly mix together all the ingredients, except the cheese and chutney, until you have a shaggy, rough dough. Cover the bowl with a clean shower cap or your choice of cover and leave the bowl on the counter for 1 hour.

Step 2: After an hour or so, perform the first set of pulls and folds until the dough feels less sticky and comes together into a soft ball. Cover the bowl again and leave it on your counter.

Step 3: Over the next few hours, do three more sets of pulls and folds on the dough, covering the dough after each set. Perform the final set before going to bed.

Step 4: Leave the covered bowl on the counter overnight, typically 8 to 10 hours, at 64 to 68°F (18 to 20°C).

Step 5: In the morning, the dough will have grown to double in size, with a smooth surface. Sprinkle flour over your kitchen counter and lay the pan liner open alongside the dough. Using a bowl scraper or your hands, gently ease the risen dough from the bowl onto the counter. Use your fingertips to start stretching and pushing out the dough, until it becomes a 7½ x 15¾–inch (19 x 40–cm) rectangle with an even thickness all over (see Top Tip). The dough will want to pull back as your stretch it; continue to pull it gently, being careful not to make holes in the dough.

Sprinkle the cubed cheese evenly over the stretchy dough and dot teaspoonfuls of the chutney across the cheese. Roll up the dough from one of the shorter edges toward the other to make an even roll of dough. Lift the sausage of dough and place it on the paper liner, then use the paper to lift it into the sandwich pan. Cover the pan with your shower cap or cover, and allow it to proof again on the counter until the dough has grown up to level with the pan edge.

Step 6: When you are ready to bake, decide whether you would like to bake in a preheated oven or from a cold start. If preheating, set the oven to 350°F (180°C) convection or 400°F (200°C) conventional.

If you preheated the oven, bake uncovered for 40 minutes. If using a cold start, place the uncovered pan of dough in the oven, set the temperature as directed and set a timer for 45 minutes.

Step 7: Remove the loaf from the oven and the pan, remove the paper, tap the base of the loaf and if it sounds hollow, the loaf is baked. If not, return it to the oven, out of the pan, directly onto the rack to bake for a further 5 to 10 minutes. Remove the loaf from the oven and allow it to cool on a wire rack for at least an hour before slicing.

Top Tip:

When you stretch out the dough in Step 5, stretch out the width to match the length of the loaf pan you will be using to bake it in. It makes it easier to ensure it is the right size for the pan.

Chickpea, Barberry and Lemon Pantry Loaf

Who doesn't have a can of chickpeas or beans lurking in their cupboard? Or various leftover ingredients from recipes they have made but never needed again? The aim of this recipe is to show that you can open your kitchen cupboard, peek in and grab whatever you find and add it to a dough. You may even find that you create a new family favorite this way.

In my loaf, the preserved lemon adds a superb, subtle flavor; the dried barberries give it bursts of sourness; and the chickpeas within the loaf are soft and any poking out of the crust provide a roasted crunch. Yours could include other beans instead, and a choice of seeds, herbs, spices, chutneys, sauces . . . the possibilities are endless.

PREP: Feed your starter to generate the 50 grams (¼ cup) of active starter needed for the recipe; see page 18 for full details. Prepare a round banneton, 8¾ inches (22 cm) in diameter and 3¼ inches (8.5 cm) deep, or a lined bowl, with rice flour and set aside a large baking pan with a lid, plus parchment paper.

Makes 1 standard loaf

50 g (¼ cup) active starter

350 g (1½ cups) water

500 g (4 cups) strong white bread flour

100 g (½ cup) drained home-cooked or canned chickpeas

30 g (⅛ cup) dried barberries (see Top Tip)

30 g (⅛ cup) preserved lemon peel (from 1 lemon), chopped, or 2 tsp (4 g) grated lemon zest

2 g (1 tsp) ground cumin

7 g (1 tsp) salt, or to taste

Rice flour, for dusting

Step 1: In the early evening, in a large mixing bowl, roughly mix together all the ingredients, except the rice flour, until you have a shaggy, lumpy, rough dough. Cover the bowl with a clean shower cap or your choice of cover and leave the bowl on the counter for 1 hour.

Step 2: After an hour or so, perform the first set of pulls and folds until the dough feels less sticky and comes together into a soft ball. You will feel the fillings in the dough, but you will still be able to stretch the dough. Cover the bowl again and leave it on your counter.

Step 3: Over the next few hours, do three more sets of pulls and folds on the dough, covering the dough after each set. Perform the final set before going to bed.

Step 4: Leave the covered bowl on the counter overnight, typically 8 to 10 hours, at 64 to 68°F (18 to 20°C).

Step 5: In the morning, the dough will have grown to double, almost triple in size. Gently but firmly perform a final set of pulls and folds on the dough to pull it into a ball. The dough will be bouncy and have a satisfying resistance you will be able to feel. Place the dough, smooth side down, in the banneton, cover with the same shower cap and place in the fridge for at least 3 hours.

Chickpea, Barberry and Lemon Pantry Loaf (Continued)

Step 6: When you are ready to bake, decide whether you would like to bake in a preheated oven or from a cold start. If preheating, set the oven to 425°F (220°C) convection or 450°F (230°C) conventional.

Remove the cover from the banneton, then place the paper over the top of the banneton and the pan upside down over the top of them both. With one hand under the banneton and one on the pan, turn it all over together to turn the dough out of the banneton and into the pan. Score the dome of dough.

If you preheated the oven, put the lid on and bake for 50 minutes. If using a cold start, place the covered pan of dough in the oven, set the temperature as directed and set a timer for 55 minutes.

After the baking time, remove the pan from the oven. Open the lid and check the loaf. If you feel that it is looking pale, place the pan with the loaf back in the hot oven, minus the lid, for 5 to 10 minutes to brown the loaf to the color of your choice.

Step 7: Once baked, carefully remove the loaf from the pan, saving the parchment paper for next time, and allow the baked loaf to cool on a wire rack for at least an hour before slicing.

Top Tip:

Replace the dried barberries with dried cranberries for a sweet-tart burst.

Roasted Vegetable and Harissa Fridge Raid Loaf

Leftovers are my joy, I often prefer leftovers to the actual meal because they have had time for the flavors to develop, and can be the basis of an array of wonderful meals. And as is my way, I have great fun seeing what lies in my fridge and can be added to a dough, which is how this loaf was created. The roasted carrot and red onion create pockets of flavor bursts, while the harissa adds an overall pleasing warmth without being a sharp heat.

You could use 200 grams (1¼ cups) of any leftover vegetables you have, plus any sauces or preserves you have tucked away. Sweet potato and butternut squash also would work well. What's in your fridge that could enhance your next dough?

PREP: Feed your starter to generate the 50 grams (¼ cup) of active starter needed for the recipe; see page 18 for full details. Prepare a round banneton, 8¾ inches (22 cm) in diameter and 3¼ inches (8.5 cm) deep, or a similarly sized bowl, with rice flour and set aside a large baking pan with a lid, plus parchment paper.

Makes 1 standard loaf

50 g (¼ cup) active starter

350 g (1½ cups) water

500 g (4 cups) strong white bread flour

200 g (1¼ cups) leftover roasted carrot and red onion (see Top Tip)

28 g (2 tbsp) harissa (double the amount if you like a hotter spice)

7 g (1 tsp) salt, or to taste

Rice flour, for dusting

Step 1: In the early evening, in a large mixing bowl, roughly mix together all the ingredients, except the rice flour, until you have a sticky, color-streaked, rough dough. Cover the bowl with a clean shower cap or your choice of cover and leave the bowl on the counter for 1 hour.

Step 2: After an hour or so, perform the first set of pulls and folds; the dough with be heavy but stretchy around the vegetables, and will come into a soft ball. Cover the bowl again and leave it on your counter.

Step 3: Over the next few hours, do three more sets of pulls and folds on the dough, covering the dough after each set. The dough will become orange from the harissa and be stretchier with each handling. Stop when the dough comes into a soft ball. Perform the final set before going to bed.

Step 4: Leave the covered bowl on the counter overnight, typically 8 to 10 hours, at 64 to 68°F (18 to 20°C).

Step 5: In the morning, the dough will have grown to double, almost triple in size, with a bumpy surface. Gently but firmly perform a final set of pulls and folds on the dough to pull it into a ball. The dough will be bouncy and have a satisfying resistance you will be able to feel. Place the dough, smooth side down, in the banneton, cover with the same shower cap and place in the fridge for at least 3 hours, up to 24 hours.

(continued)

Step 6: When you are ready to bake, decide whether you would like to bake in a preheated oven or from a cold start. If preheating, set the oven to 425°F (220°C) convection or 450°F (230°C) conventional.

Remove the cover from the banneton, then place the paper over the top of the banneton and the pan upside down over the top of them both. With one hand under the banneton and one on the pan, turn it all over together to turn the dough out of the banneton and into the pan. Score the dome of dough.

If you preheated the oven, put the lid on and bake for 50 minutes. If using a cold start, place the covered pan of dough in the oven, set the temperature as directed and set a timer for 55 minutes.

After the baking time for either option, remove the covered pan from the oven. Open the lid to check the loaf. Baking in a lidded pan produces a golden loaf. When you take the lid off, if you feel that your loaf is looking pale, place it back in the hot oven, in its pan, minus the lid, for 5 to 10 minutes to brown the loaf to the color of your choice.

Step 7: Once baked, carefully remove the loaf from the pan, saving the parchment paper for next time, and allow the baked loaf to cool on a wire rack for at least an hour before slicing. The baked loaf will smell wonderful!

Top Tip:

If your carrot and onion, or other roasted veggies, are in large pieces, chop them into smaller sizes before adding them to the dough.

THE FLAT
Sourdough Collection

This collection of recipes uses My Master Recipe (page 33) as a base to make flatter breads, such as focaccia (page 148), pizza (page 150) and fougasse (page 156). This shows how the dough can be manipulated and shaped to make more than merely loaves. All of these recipes can be personalized according to your tastes and preferences.

These breads are all wonderful plain or you can top and fill them with the ingredients of your choice. They can all be served with a variety of meals, or as the meal, their flatness making them perfect bases for toppings or dipping.

My Master Sourdough Focaccia

Focaccia of any type is a wonderful bread to eat, and sourdough focaccia is even better—in my personal opinion, that is. For this version, I use My Master Recipe dough (page 33) and convert it to focaccia. I highly recommend not skimping on the olive oil and thoroughly enjoying dimpling the dough with your fingertips when the time comes.

NOTE: After the main or overnight proof, if you would like to bake the dough later in the day, place the bowl, untouched, still covered, with the proofed dough inside, in the fridge to halt any more growth. When you are ready to use the dough, take it from the fridge, allow it to warm up, then continue from Step 5.

PREP: Feed your starter to generate the 50 grams (¼ cup) of active starter needed for the recipe; see page 18 for full details. Have ready a medium-sized baking sheet, about 10 x 14 inches (26 x 36 cm).

Makes 1 standard loaf

50 g (¼ cup) active starter

350 g (1½ cups) water

500 g (4 cups) strong white bread flour (see Top Tip)

7 g (1 tsp) salt, or to taste

30 to 45 ml (2 to 3 tbsp) olive oil

Step 1: In the early evening, in a large mixing bowl, roughly mix together all the ingredients, except the olive oil, until you have a shaggy, rough dough. Cover the bowl with a clean shower cap or your choice of cover and leave the bowl on the counter for 1 hour.

Step 2: After an hour or so, perform the first set of pulls and folds until the dough feels less sticky and comes together into a soft ball. Cover the bowl again and leave it on your counter.

Step 3: Over the next few hours, do three more sets of pulls and folds on the dough, covering the dough after each set. Perform the final set before going to bed.

Step 4: Leave the covered bowl on the counter overnight, typically 8 to 10 hours, at 64 to 68°F (18 to 20°C).

Step 5: The next morning, the dough will have doubled in size and is now ready to be used to make focaccia. Prepare your baking sheet by liberally drizzling it with the olive oil.

Using a bowl scraper or your hands, gently ease the bubbly risen dough from the bowl onto the prepared pan. Being careful not to squash the dough too much, gently turn it over in the oil so that it is covered completely with olive oil. Cover the entire pan loosely with a large plastic bag or plastic wrap and leave it on the counter for 1½ to 2 hours.

Step 6: When you are ready to bake, decide whether you would like to bake in a preheated oven or from a cold start. If preheating, set the oven to 400°F (200°C) convection or 425°F (220°C) conventional.

Using your fingertips, firmly press dimples all over the dough, spreading it out at the same time until it fills the pan.

If you preheated the oven, bake uncovered for 20 minutes. If using a cold start, place the uncovered pan of dough in the oven, set the temperature as directed and set a timer for 25 minutes.

Step 7: Remove the baked focaccia from the oven and let it rest in the pan for 15 to 20 minutes, then ease the baked bread off the pan, transfer it to a board or large plate, cut it into pieces and serve.

Top Tip:

Replace a portion of the strong white bread flour with a whole-grain flour for a fuller flavor; note that the baked loaf will be slightly denser.

Sourdough Focaccia Pizza

Sourdoughs can be used for any bread-based dish that you would like to make, and in this case, I am using mine to make a focaccia base for a pizza-style dish. For this recipe, you can choose the thickness or thinness you would prefer for the finished pizza, and I have included tips for how to amend it. Top with your favorite pizza toppings!

PREP: Feed your starter to generate the 30 grams (⅛ cup) of active starter needed for the recipe; see page 18 for full details. Have ready a medium-sized baking sheet, about 10 x 14 inches (25 x 35 cm).

Makes 1 large pizza or 2 medium-sized pizzas

30 g (⅛ cup) active starter

225 g (scant 1 cup) water

300 g (2½ cups) strong white bread flour

3.5 g (½ tsp) salt, or to taste

Rice flour or ground semolina, for dusting

Topping Ideas

Pizza sauce of your choice

Mozzarella or other grated cheese

Fresh basil leaves

Sliced vegetables

Cooked meats of your choice

Step 1: In the early evening, in a large mixing bowl, roughly mix together all the dough ingredients, except the rice flour or semolina, until you have a shaggy, rough dough. Cover the bowl with a clean shower cap or your choice of cover and leave the bowl on the counter for 1 hour.

Step 2: After an hour or so, perform the first set of pulls and folds until the dough feels less sticky and comes together into a soft ball. Cover the bowl again and leave it on your counter.

Step 3: Over the next few hours, do three more sets of pulls and folds on the dough, covering the dough after each set. Perform the final set before going to bed.

Step 4: Leave the covered bowl on the counter overnight, typically 8 to 10 hours, at 64 to 68°F (18 to 20°C).

Step 5: The next morning, the dough will have doubled in size and is now ready to be used to make a focaccia-style pizza base. Place the bowl of proofed dough, untouched, still covered, in the fridge to halt any more growth. When you are ready to use the dough to make pizzas for lunch or dinner, take it from the fridge, allow it to warm up to room temperature for an hour, then continue.

Prepare your baking sheet by sprinkling it with a layer of rice flour or ground semolina.

Using a bowl scraper or your hands, gently ease the bubbly risen dough from the bowl onto the prepared pan—leave it unformed at this point. Cover the entire pan loosely with a large plastic bag or plastic wrap and leave it on the counter for 2 to 3 hours.

Step 6: Preheat the oven to 400°F (200°C) convection or 425°F (220°C) conventional.

Using your fingertips, firmly press the dough out to the edges and corners of the pan.

Cover the surface with the toppings of your choice. For my pizza, I used a tomato pizza sauce, mixed roasted Mediterranean vegetables and mozzarella. Bake for 18 to 20 minutes, or until the cheese has melted and the edges of the base are browned.

Step 7: Remove from the oven, ease the baked pizza off the pan and serve.

Top Tips:

If you would prefer to parbake the pizza base prior to adding toppings, or for use later, bake at the Step 6 temperature from a cold start for 20 minutes, or in a preheated oven for 15 minutes.

To use the base later, preheat the oven to 400°F (200°C) convection or 425°F (220°C) conventional, add toppings to the base and place directly on the oven rack for a crispy, crunchy base. Bake for 12 to 15 minutes in a preheated oven or 15 to 18 minutes from a cold start set to the Step 6 temperature.

Sourdough Ciabatta Loaves

These flat, holey loaves are not just picturesque; they are great for making sandwiches, as pizza bases or for eating alongside a meal. Ciabatta is made from a wetter dough to produce flat loaves or rolls full of holes ready to be filled with butter. Using sourdough to make ciabatta can seem challenging as the dough is so lively, but it is a fun dough to work with.

NOTE: After the main or overnight proof, if you would like to bake the dough later in the day, place the bowl of proofed dough, untouched, still covered, in the fridge to halt any more growth.

When you are ready to use the dough, take it from the fridge, allow it to warm up, then continue from Step 5.

PREP: Feed your starter to generate the 30 grams (⅛ cup) of active starter needed for the recipe; see page 18 for full details. For proofing, line a large, rimmed baking or cookie sheet with a clean tea towel; choose one that will fit into your fridge. For baking, you will need a large baking or cookie sheet lined with parchment paper.

Makes 2 medium-sized loaves

30 g (⅛ cup) active starter

225 g (scant 1 cup) water

300 g (2½ cups) strong white bread flour

3.5 g (½ tsp) salt, or to taste

Rice flour, for dusting

Step 1: In the early evening, in a large mixing bowl, roughly mix together all the ingredients, except the rice flour, until you have a shaggy, rough dough. Cover the bowl with a clean shower cap or your choice of cover and leave the bowl on the counter for 1 hour.

Step 2: After an hour or so, perform the first set of pulls and folds until the dough feels less sticky and comes together into a soft ball; the ball will hold its shape briefly only. Cover the bowl again and leave it on your counter.

Step 3: Over the next few hours, do three more sets of pulls and folds on the dough, covering the dough after each set. This will be a soft, lively dough that will come into a loose ball each time. Perform the final set before going to bed.

Step 4: Leave the covered bowl on the counter overnight, typically 8 to 10 hours, at 64 to 68°F (18 to 20°C).

Step 5: In the morning, the dough will have grown to double, almost triple in size.

Sprinkle your tea towel—lined rimmed baking sheet generously with rice flour.

(continued)

Sourdough Ciabatta Loaves (Continued)

Next, sprinkle your counter generously with rice flour. Gently turn your dough out from the bowl onto the counter. Cut it equally, by eye, into two pieces.

Using the same pulls and folds method, pull each portion of dough into a soft parcel, then turn one half over into itself and roll it gently into a plump sausage. Place the dough, smooth side down, on the counter. Use your fingertips to pull and push the dough into a 12 x 3–inch (30 x 8–cm) oval. Carefully lift each piece and place it on the prepared tea towel and sprinkle the top with rice flour. Cover with a clean, damp tea towel or large plastic bag and leave on the counter for 2 to 3 hours to proof again.

Once the dough has puffed up to double the thickness, place the baking sheet with its proofed dough into your fridge while you preheat the oven, to firm up. This will make it easier to handle the dough.

Step 6: To bake, preheat the oven to 400°F (200°C) convection or 425°F (220°C) conventional.

Remove the pan of the proofed dough from the fridge and gently lift the doughs onto your parchment-lined baking sheet, turning them over so that they are smooth side up. Bake for 16 to 20 minutes, or until puffed up and browned.

Step 7: Once baked, allow to cool briefly before eating.

After the main overnight proof, have everything ready to prepare your dough.

Turn the dough out onto a floured surface and cut it into two pieces.

Use pulls and folds to pull each piece into a ball.

Roll the balls into ovals or fat sausages.

Push the pieces out to flat ovals; the dough will bounce back but keep going.

Lay each long flattened piece onto a floured tea towel; cover and proof again then bake as per the recipe.

Sourdough Cheesy Fougasse

Fougasse is a leaf-shaped and scored flatbread. It is another way to use sourdough, by stretching and shaping and scoring the dough and baking it to a thinner, crunchy finish. Part of the fun of making fougasse is creating the shape and cuts in the dough. This does not need to follow a standard pattern; you can get as creative as you like! I have used finely grated Parmesan on this fougasse. Feel free to use your favorite cheese, or a mixture of two or three, and add as much as you fancy.

NOTE: After the main or overnight proof, if you would like to bake the dough later in the day, place the bowl of proofed dough, untouched, still covered, in the fridge to halt any more growth. When you are ready to use the dough, take it from the fridge, allow it to warm up, then continue from Step 5.

PREP: Feed your starter to generate the 30 grams (⅛ cup) of active starter needed for the recipe; see page 18 for full details. For the second proofing and baking, have ready two large baking or cookie sheets lined with parchment paper.

Makes 2 fougasse

30 g (⅛ cup) active starter

210 g (¾ cup plus 2 tbsp) water

300 g (2½ cups) strong white bread flour

20 g (1 tbsp) olive oil

3.5 g (½ tsp) salt, or to taste

Rice flour or ground semolina, for dusting

20 g (2 tbsp) finely grated Parmesan cheese, for topping

Step 1: In the early evening, in a large mixing bowl, roughly mix together all the ingredients, except the rice flour or semolina and Parmesan, until you have a shaggy, rough dough. Cover the bowl with a clean shower cap or your choice of cover and leave the bowl on the counter for 1 hour.

Step 2: After an hour or so, perform the first set of pulls and folds until the dough feels less sticky and comes together into a soft ball. Cover the bowl again and leave it on your counter.

Step 3: Over the next few hours, do three more sets of pulls and folds on the dough, covering the dough after each set. Perform the final set before going to bed.

Step 4: Leave the covered bowl on the counter overnight, typically 8 to 10 hours, at 64 to 68°F (18 to 20°C).

Step 5: In the morning, the dough will have grown to double, almost triple in size.

Sprinkle the paper lining of your prepared baking sheets with rice flour or ground semolina. Next, sprinkle your counter generously with rice flour. Gently turn your dough out from the bowl onto the counter. Cut it equally, by eye, into two pieces.

Using the same pulls and folds method, pull each portion of dough into a soft parcel, then turn one half over into itself and roll it gently into a plump sausage. Use your fingertips to pull and push the pieces of dough into a 12 by 10–inch (30 x 25–cm) oval. The dough will want to bounce back and resist being stretched; if that is the case, allow it to rest for 5 to 10 minutes, then continue to stretch it. Carefully lift each piece and place it on a prepared baking sheet. Using a pizza cutter, cut one line down the middle of the dough and shorter diagonal cuts on either side to represent a leaf design. Cover the pan with a large plastic bag and leave on the counter to proof again for 2 to 3 hours, or until the dough has puffed up to double the thickness.

Step 6: To bake, preheat the oven to 400°F (200°C) convection or 425°F (220°C) conventional. Sprinkle the Parmesan evenly across both breads and bake uncovered for 18 to 20 minutes, or until puffed up and browned.

Step 7: Once baked, allow to cool briefly before eating.

Top Tip:

Try making an herb variation by adding 2 grams (2 tsp) dried rosemary or the herb of your choice when mixing the dough. You can use the herbs either in addition to or in place of the Parmesan.

THE SHAPED
Collection

I thoroughly enjoy playing with dough. I like to see how it can be manipulated and used to create something unexpected, or to take sourdough from being the standard idea of a white crusty loaf to something dramatic or fun that enhances any dinner table.

Sourdough can literally be whatever you want it to be. When you are faced with a wobbly bowl of dough, that may not seem to be the case, but I can guide you in some ideas for using this vivacious dough to make tasty sculptures that you may not have thought possible. The methods and shapes in this collection may also inspire you to try using some of the other loaf doughs in this book in other ways.

Master Recipe Baby Braided Loaf

I think there is nothing more fun than playing with dough and seeing what happens; my braided loaves were a result of doing just that. This recipe uses my Baby Master Loaf–size dough (page 72) with an extra tweak before being baked. These loaves are a great addition to any table. Also, in this dough I have used Khorasan flour; if you cannot find it where you are, use whole wheat flour instead. No other changes will be necessary.

PREP: Feed your starter to generate the 30 grams (⅛ cup) of active starter needed for the recipe; see page 18 for full details. Prepare a round banneton, 6¾ inches (17 cm) in diameter and 3¼ inches (8.5 cm) deep, or a lined bowl, with rice flour, and set aside a large baking pan with a lid, plus parchment paper. You will also need a rolling pin and dough knife or bowl scraper.

Makes 1 small loaf

30 g (⅛ cup) active starter

210 g (scant 1 cup) water

200 g (1½ cups) strong white bread flour

100 g (1 cup) Khorasan or whole wheat flour

4 g (½ tsp) salt, or to taste

Rice flour, for dusting

*See step-by-step pictures on page 162.

Step 1: In the early evening, in a large mixing bowl, roughly mix together all the ingredients, except the rice flour, until you have a shaggy, rough dough. Cover the bowl with a clean shower cap or your choice of cover and leave the bowl on the counter for 1 hour.

Step 2: After an hour or so, perform the first set of pulls and folds until the dough feels less sticky and comes together into a soft ball. Cover the bowl again and leave it on your counter.

Step 3: Over the next few hours, do three more sets of pulls and folds on the dough, covering the dough after each set. Perform the final set before going to bed.

Step 4: Leave the covered bowl on the counter overnight, typically 8 to 10 hours, at 64 to 68°F (18 to 20°C).

Step 5: In the morning, the dough will have grown to double, almost triple in size. Gently but firmly perform a final set of pulls and folds on the dough to pull it into a ball. The dough will have a good structured feel. Place the dough, smooth side down, in the banneton, sprinkle extra rice flour down the sides and across the surface, cover with the same shower cap and place in the fridge for at least 3 hours, maximum 24 hours.

Step 6: When you are ready to bake, decide whether you would like to bake in a preheated oven or from a cold start. If preheating, set the oven to 425°F (220°C) convection or 450°F (230°C) conventional. Remove the cover from the banneton, sprinkle your counter with rice flour and gently turn the dough out onto the counter. Have the parchment paper within easy reach in readiness.

Using a rolling pin, flatten out equal portions from three equally spaced points of the dough to create three pieces, sticking out from the sides of the dough. Cut each flattened portion along its length into three strips, still attached at the base. Braid each piece, then lift them up and across the dome to meet in the middle. See images on the next page. Lift the dough onto the parchment paper and lift it with the paper into your pan.

If you preheated the oven, put the lid on the pan and bake for 45 minutes. If using a cold start, place the covered pan of dough in the oven, set the temperature as directed and set a timer for 50 minutes.

After the baking time for either option, remove the covered pan from the oven. Open the lid to check the loaf. Baking in a lidded pan produces a golden loaf. When you take the lid off, if you feel that your loaf is looking pale, place it back in the hot oven, in its pan, minus the lid, for 5 to 10 minutes to brown the loaf to the color of your choice.

Step 7: Once baked, carefully remove the loaf from the pan, saving the parchment paper for next time, and allow the baked loaf to cool on a wire rack for at least an hour before slicing.

Top Tip:

To convert this recipe to bake a full-size loaf, use 50 grams (¼ cup) active starter, 350 grams (1½ cups) of water, 350 grams (2½ cups) of strong white bread flour, 150 grams (1½ cups) of Khorasan or whole wheat flour and 7 grams (1 tsp) of salt, or to taste. Follow the same directions for making and braiding the dough, and bake for an additional 5 to 10 minutes.

Master Recipe Baby Braided Loaf (Continued)

When you are ready to bake, gently turn the dough onto a floured surface; have your rolling pin, pan and dough knife or a sharp knife ready.

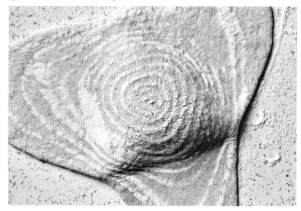

Push into the dome of dough with the rolling pin on three sides and roll out three equal tongues of dough.

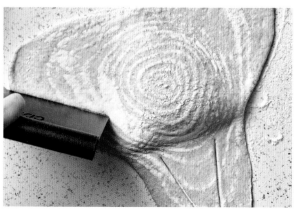

Use the dough knife or sharp knife to cut each tongue into three pieces.

Braid each of the three pieces.

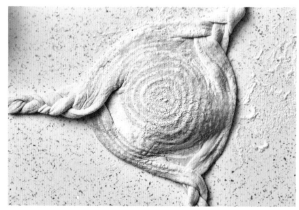

Squeeze the ends of each braid together to hold it together, then lift each one across the dough to meet in the middle.

Twist the ends of the braids together on the top, then lift the whole dough into your lined pan and bake as per the recipe.

Chocolate and Nut Sourdough Crown

This sweet and crunchy sourdough crown is fit for an afternoon tea, a dessert, an event or for no reason whatsoever other than because it is so good! Use any nuts of your choice, or seeds if you prefer. I have used Nutella® for the chocolate spread; feel free to use an alternative of your choice.

This is wonderful to eat freshly baked and slightly warm; the next day, it is equally good and even better if you warm it slightly to soften the bread and chocolate spread. Thirty seconds in a microwave works perfectly.

PREP: Feed your starter to generate the 30 grams (⅛ cup) of active starter needed for the recipe; see page 18 for full details. Line a large baking or cookie sheet with parchment paper.

Makes 1 medium-sized bread crown

30 g (⅛ cup) active starter

110 g (½ cup) water

110 g (½ cup) milk of your choice

300 g (2½ cups) strong white bread flour, plus more for dusting

4 g (½ tsp) salt, or to taste

Mix-Ins

100 g (Ð cup) chocolate spread

80 g (½ cup) chopped nuts

Step 1: In the early evening, in a large mixing bowl, roughly mix together all the ingredients, except the chocolate spread and nuts, until you have a shaggy dough. Cover the bowl with a clean shower cap or your choice of cover and leave the bowl on the counter for 1 hour.

Step 2: After an hour or so, perform the first set of pulls and folds until the dough feels less sticky and comes together into a soft ball. This dough will quickly become tight due to the milk in the dough. Cover the bowl again and leave it on your counter.

Step 3: Over the next few hours, do three more sets of pulls and folds on the dough until the dough comes into a ball each time, covering the dough after each set. It will take fewer and fewer actions to pull it into a ball each time. Perform the final set before going to bed.

Step 4: Leave the covered bowl on the counter overnight, typically 8 to 10 hours, at 64 to 68°F (18 to 20°C).

Step 5: In the morning, the dough will have grown to double in size with a smooth surface. Sprinkle flour over your kitchen counter. Using a bowl scraper or your hands, gently ease the risen dough from the bowl onto the counter. Use your fingertips to start stretching and pushing out the dough until it becomes a 12 x 10–inch (30 x 25–cm) rectangle with an even thickness all over. The dough will want to pull back as you stretch it; continue to pull it gently, being careful not to make holes in the dough.

(continued)

Chocolate and Nut Sourdough Crown (Continued)

Spread the chocolate spread evenly over the stretchy dough; if the spread is warmed slightly, it may be easier to spread without pulling on the dough. Sprinkle the chopped nuts evenly over the top, right up to the edges. Roll up the dough from one of the longer edges toward the other to make an even roll of dough. Pull the sausage into a circle, sticking the ends together. The circle should be around 8 inches (20 cm) in diameter with a 3-inch (8-cm) hole in the middle.

Place the circle of dough on your prepared baking sheet. Cover the whole pan with a large reused plastic bag and leave it on the counter to proof again for 2 to 3 hours.

Step 6: When you are ready to bake, decide whether you would like to bake in a preheated oven or from a cold start. If preheating, set the oven to 360°F (180°C) convection or 400°F (200°C) conventional.

Using a bowl scraper, dough knife or sharp knife, make twelve evenly spaced cuts into the circumference of the dough circle, nearly all of the way through the dough, but leaving the circle intact in the middle. Turn each cut portion slightly to one side, all in the same direction going around.

If you preheated the oven, bake uncovered for 20 to 25 minutes. If using a cold start, place the uncovered pan of dough in the oven, set the temperature as directed and set a timer for 25 to 30 minutes.

Step 7: Remove the loaf from the oven and the pan. Allow the loaf to cool briefly on a wire rack so that you can handle it and it is not too hot to eat, then serve. It is best eaten warm!

Top Tip:

Once cooled, refresh in the oven briefly to soften the bread and make the chocolate spread gooey again. Set your oven to 360°F (180°C) convection or 400°F (200°C) conventional. Place the bread on a baking sheet and heat in the oven for 5 to 6 minutes.

Pull-Apart Sharing Sesame Sourdough

Making bread to share is one of the things I enjoy the most about baking sourdough, and pull-apart loaves are the epitome of sharing. These bakes are also fun to make and can lead you to try your own ideas and tweaks. Enjoy playing and creating shapes of your own.

I have used standard light brown sesame seeds in this recipe, but these could be swapped out for black sesame seeds, flaxseeds or sunflower seeds.

PREP: Feed your starter to generate the 50 grams (¼ cup) of active starter needed for the recipe; see page 18 for full details. Prepare a round banneton, 8¾ inches (22 cm) in diameter and 3¼ inches (8.5 cm) deep, or a lined bowl, with rice flour, and have ready a large baking sheet, and parchment paper cut to the same size.

Makes 1 standard loaf

50 g (¼ cup) active starter

350 g (1½ cups) water

500 g (4 cups) strong white bread flour

7 g (1 tsp) salt, or to taste

50 g (¼ cup) raw sesame seeds

Rice flour, for dusting

Step 1: In the early evening, in a large mixing bowl, roughly mix together all the ingredients except the sesame seeds and rice flour, until you have a shaggy, rough dough. Cover the bowl with a clean shower cap or your choice of cover and leave the bowl on the counter for 1 hour.

Step 2: After an hour or so, perform the first set of pulls and folds until the dough feels less sticky and comes together into a soft ball. Cover the bowl again and leave it on your counter.

Step 3: Over the next few hours, do three more sets of pulls and folds on the dough, covering the dough after each set. Perform the final set before going to bed.

Step 4: Leave the covered bowl on the counter overnight, typically 8 to 10 hours, at 64 to 68°F (18 to 20°C).

Step 5: In the morning, the dough will have grown to double, almost triple in size. Place the sesame seeds in a medium-sized bowl.

Gently but firmly perform a final set of pulls and folds on the dough to pull it into a ball. The dough will be bouncy and have a satisfying resistance you will be able to feel. Lift it and roll it in the sesame seeds; they will stick easily.

Place the dough, smooth side down, in the banneton, adding the leftover sesame seeds down the sides and over the top of the dough. Cover with the same shower cap and place in the fridge for at least 3 to 24 hours.

Step 6: When you are ready to bake, decide whether you would like to bake in a preheated oven or from a cold start. If preheating, set the oven to 350°F (180°C) convection or 400°F (200°C) conventional.

Place a sheet of parchment paper on your counter and sprinkle it with a layer of rice flour. Remove the cover from the banneton and gently turn the dome of dough onto the floured paper. Using a dough knife, or the sharp edge of a bowl scraper, cut into the dough in twelve equally spaced cuts going around, 3½ inches (9 cm) from the outer edge. Do not cut all the way across the dough; leave a circle uncut in the middle.

Gently separate each cut, then twist each "triangle" upward, all in the same direction, so that the peak or corner of each section stands up.

Gently lift the paper with the dough onto your ready baking sheet.

If you preheated the oven, bake uncovered for 30 to 35 minutes. If using a cold start, place the uncovered pan of dough in the oven, set the temperature as directed and set a timer for 35 to 40 minutes, or until the sesame seeds are nicely browned and aromatic.

Step 7: Once baked, carefully remove the loaf from the pan, and briefly allow the baked loaf to cool on a wire rack before serving.

Top Tip:

Prior to Step 6, place the banneton full of dough into the freezer for 30 minutes before turning it out; this will help the dough to firm up and make it easier to handle.

Cheesy Sourdough Twisted Crown

This attractive crown bursting with melted cheese is created by filling, rolling, cutting and twisting the dough. This recipe and process are open to lots of filling options; including different colored additions will only enhance the crown's appearance. The whole wheat flour in this recipe complements the cheese and produces a firm dough, making it easier to handle and work with.

PREP: Feed your starter to generate the 50 grams (¼ cup) of active starter needed for the recipe; see page 18 for full details. Line a large baking or cookie sheet with parchment paper.

Makes 1 large crown

50 g (¼ cup) active starter

350 g (1½ cups) water

300 g (2½ cups) strong white bread flour, plus more for dusting

200 g (1¾ cups) whole wheat flour

7 g (1 tsp) salt, or to taste

150 g (1 cup) grated hard cheese of your choice (I like sharp Cheddar)

Step 1: In the early evening, in a large mixing bowl, roughly mix together all the ingredients, minus the cheese, until you have a shaggy, rough dough; this will be an easy mix. Cover the bowl with a clean shower cap or your choice of cover and leave the bowl on the counter for 1 hour.

Step 2: After an hour or so, perform the first set of pulls and folds until the dough feels less sticky and comes together into a soft ball; the dough will be stretchy from the whole wheat flour. Cover the bowl again and leave it on your counter.

Step 3: Over the next few hours, do three more sets of pulls and folds on the dough, covering the dough after each set. Perform the final set before going to bed.

Step 4: Leave the covered bowl on the counter overnight, typically 8 to 10 hours, at 64 to 68°F (18 to 20°C).

Step 5: In the morning, the dough will have grown to double in size with a smooth surface. Turn the dough out onto a floured surface. Have your pan ready and place the flattened paper liner on the counter.

Pull and stretch the dough into a 12 x 15¾–inch (30 x 40–cm) rectangle. This will be a firm dough and easy to control. Sprinkle the grated cheese evenly across the surface from edge to edge. Firmly roll the dough from one long side to the other into a sausage.

Once rolled, use a dough knife or sharp knife to cut the sausage lengthwise down the middle into two equal pieces. Twist the two pieces around each other and into an 8-inch (20-cm) circle. Lift the circle of dough onto the paper, then lift it all onto the pan. Cover the pan with a large bag or clean, damp tea towel and proof again for 2 to 3 hours, or until it has grown to one and a half times its size.

Step 6: When you are ready to bake, decide whether you would like to bake in a preheated oven or from a cold start. If preheating, set the oven to 360°F (180°C) convection or 400°F (200°C) conventional.

If you preheated the oven, bake uncovered for 35 to 40 minutes. If using a cold start, place the uncovered pan of dough in the oven, set the temperature as directed and set a timer for 40 to 45 minutes. If the cheese begins to brown too much, cover the loaf with an upside-down pan.

Step 7: Once baked, carefully remove the round from the pan and briefly allow it to cool on a rack before serving. It is best eaten warm, but can also be reheated to eat later.

Top Tip:

Once cooled, refresh in the oven briefly to soften the bread and make the cheese melt and bubble again. Preheat your oven to 360°F (180°C) convection or 400°F (200°C) conventional. Place the bread on a baking sheet and heat in the oven for 10 to 15 minutes.

My Sourdough Baguettes

This recipe uses My Master Recipe dough (page 33) shaped to make baguettes with crusty, crunchy exteriors and soft, holey interiors. To make these, I use baguette bannetons, or sometimes a perforated baguette pan, or sometimes shape and proof them on a cloth sprinkled with rice flour. In the recipe, I am using my baguette banneton, but if you have a preferred way of shaping yours, feel free to use it with my dough.

Try a variation on the baguettes by adding 150 grams (1¼ cups) of cooked and cooled grains, such as spelt, einkorn or quinoa, to the dough for extra chew and flavor; no other changes need to be made to the recipe and ingredients.

Prep: Feed your starter to generate the 30 grams (⅛ cup) of active starter needed for the recipe; see page 18 for full details. Prepare two baguette bannetons, 13 inches (33 cm) long, with rice flour. Line a large baking or cookie sheet with parchment paper.

Makes 2 medium-sized baguettes

30 g (⅛ cup) active starter

210 g (¾ cup plus 2 tbsp) water (see Top Tip)

300 g (2½ cups) strong white bread flour, plus more for dusting

4 g (½ tsp) salt, or to taste

Rice flour, for dusting

6 ice cubes

Step 1: In the early evening, in a large mixing bowl, roughly mix together all the ingredients, except the rice flour and ice cubes, until you have a shaggy, rough dough. Cover the bowl with a clean shower cap or your choice of cover and leave the bowl on the counter for 1 hour.

Step 2: After an hour or so, perform the first set of pulls and folds until the dough feels less sticky and comes together into a soft ball. Cover the bowl again and leave it on your counter.

Step 3: Over the next few hours, do three more sets of pulls and folds on the dough, covering the dough after each set. Perform the final set before going to bed.

Step 4: Leave the covered bowl on the counter overnight, typically 8 to 10 hours, at 64 to 68°F (18 to 20°C).

Step 5: In the morning, the dough will have grown to double in size.

When you are ready, sprinkle your counter generously with rice flour. Gently turn your dough out from the bowl onto the counter. Cut it equally, by eye, into two pieces.

Using the same pulls and folds method, pull each portion of dough into a soft parcel, then turn one half over into itself and roll it gently into a plump sausage. Using your palms, roll each sausage of dough to be 10 inches (25 cm) long.

(continued)

My Sourdough Baguettes (Continued)

Gently lift and place each dough sausage into a floured banneton. Cover again with shower caps or damp tea towels and place them on the counter for 2 to 3 hours, or until puffed up and doubled in size.

Step 6: When you are ready to bake, preheat the oven to 400°F (200°C) convection or 425°F (220°C) conventional and place an empty ovenproof pan on a rack at the bottom of the oven.

Once the oven is ready, place the six ice cubes on a small plate. Gently turn the baguettes onto your prepared baking sheet. Score each dough, three times diagonally, with a quick motion, or snip with scissors.

Place the pan in the hot oven, and at the same time tip the ice cubes into the hot empty pan at the bottom of the oven. Bake uncovered for a total of 18 to 20 minutes, or until nicely risen and browning.

Note:

If you use a perforated baguette baking pan, reduce the baking time by 5 minutes.

Step 7: Once baked, carefully remove the loaves from the oven and allow the baked baguettes to cool on a rack briefly before serving. They are best eaten freshly baked.

Top Tip:

Once you are happy with this recipe, try increasing the water by 15 grams (1 tbsp) and see how it affects the baked breads; as you become comfortable with handling the dough, increasing the amount of water can enhance the baked baguettes.

Turn the dough onto a floured surface, cut it into two pieces and use pulls and folds to make two balls of dough.

Have your equipment ready and shape the balls into ovals.

Roll each oval of dough into a longer sausage to fit your banneton or tray.

Cover the doughs again to proof then bake as per the recipe.

THE SAME DAY
Collection

One of the beauties of making sourdough for me is the time it takes to fully proof and develop. There is a mindful beauty to the slowness of the dough growth. However, there are times when you may wish to be able to make something sourdough-based faster. The aim of this set of recipes is to be able to make your dough, fully proof it and bake it the same day.

The key to making this work is using more starter than usual plus warm water in the dough, both of which help to make the dough start to develop immediately. Then, increasing and maintaining the heat at which the dough proofs enables you to control the proofing time.

STARTER: Feed your starter to generate the necessary amount of active starter needed for the recipe either the night before using cold water, or early in the morning using warm water, and placing it in a warm place to respond, or use your starter directly from the fridge without feeding if you have enough and if it has been fed within the last 2 weeks. Feed it once you have removed what you need to return it to your base amount.

LOCATION: Use a warm place to proof the dough. I use my oven with the pilot light on and the door propped open, which creates an even temperature of 77°F (25°C). Alternatively, use a proofing box.

Same Day Sunflower Seed Baby Loaf

This recipe utilizes my Baby Master Loaf recipe size (page 72) and allows you to be able to prepare and bake a loaf within several hours, ready for a late lunch or dinner—or ready for the next day. I have added a sunflower seed crust to this loaf to give it a tasty extra crunch; this is optional and can also be done to any of the baby loaves in this book.

TIMETABLE: To plan to make these, allow 5 to 6 hours from start to finish from the time that your starter is ready to use.

PREP: Refer to the chapter introduction on page 175 for details about how to prepare your starter for this recipe, and choosing a warm place for proofing. Prepare a round banneton, 6¾ inches (17 cm) in diameter and 3¼ inches (8.5 cm) deep, or a lined bowl, with rice flour, and set aside a large baking or cookie sheet, plus parchment paper.

Makes 1 small loaf

60 g (¼ cup plus 1 tbsp) active starter

180 g (¾ cup) warm water, around 100°F (38°C)

300 g (2½ cups) strong white bread flour

4 g (½ tsp) salt, or to taste

50 g (¼ cup) raw sunflower seeds

Step 1: In a large mixing bowl, roughly mix together all the ingredients, except the sunflower seeds, until you have a shaggy, rough dough. Cover the bowl with a clean shower cap or your choice of cover and leave the bowl in your chosen warm spot. The dough will be sticky.

Step 2: Perform the first set of pulls and folds by literally lifting a small handful of dough from one side of the bowl, stretching it up and across the rest of the dough. Turn the bowl slightly and repeat as many times as is necessary until the dough feels less sticky and comes together into a soft ball. This will be a warm soft dough. Cover the bowl again and place it back in the warmth.

Step 3: Perform the next set of pulls and folds, repeating the same actions again; the dough should be nice and stretchy and bouncy, and it should come together into a nice smooth, soft ball. Place the covered bowl back in the warmth.

Step 4: Perform the last set of pulls and folds; the dough should come together into a nice, smooth, bouncy ball. Place the covered bowl back in the warmth for the next 3 hours.

Step 5: By now, the dough should have grown to at least double its original size. It may be soft from the warm proofing, but it should not be floppy. Place the sunflowers seeds in a medium-sized bowl.

Gently but firmly perform a final set of pulls and folds on the dough to pull it into a ball. Lift it and roll it gently in the sunflower seeds.

(continued)

Place the dough, smooth side down, in the prepared banneton, sprinkle the remaining seeds down the sides and across the top of the dough, cover with the same shower cap and place in the coldest part of your fridge for at least 1 hour.

Step 6: When you are ready to bake, decide whether you would like to bake in a preheated oven or from a cold start. If preheating, set the oven to 425°F (220°C) convection or 450°F (230°C) conventional.

Remove the cover from the banneton, then place the paper over the top of the banneton and the pan upside down over the top of them both. With one hand under the banneton and one on the pan, turn it all over together to turn the dough out of the banneton and into the pan. Score the dome of dough through the seeds. This dough will be softer than a standard dough.

If you preheated the oven, put the lid on the pan and bake for 40 minutes. If using a cold start, place the covered pan of dough in the oven, set the temperature as directed and set a timer for 45 minutes.

After the baking time for either option, remove the covered pan from the oven. Open the lid to check the loaf. Baking in a lidded pan produces a golden loaf. When you take the lid off, if you feel that your loaf is looking pale, place it back in the hot oven, in its pan, minus the lid, for 5 to 10 minutes to brown the loaf to the color of your choice.

Step 7: Once baked, carefully remove the loaf from the pan, saving the parchment paper for next time, and allow the baked loaf to cool on a wire rack for at least an hour before slicing.

Top Tip:

To convert this dough to my simplest wedge rolls, refer to the Baby Master Wedge Rolls recipe (page 74) and follow the process from Step 5 onward.

Same Day Sourdough Pizzas

This recipe uses heat and more starter than my standard pizza recipe on page 150, to be able to make sourdough pizza within a day instead of including the longer overnight proof. With this recipe, you can choose to make a thin or thicker base, whichever you prefer.

TIMETABLE: To plan to make these, allow 5 to 6 hours from start to finish from the time that your starter is ready to use.

PREP: Refer to the chapter introduction on page 175 for details about how to prepare your starter for this recipe, and choosing a warm place for proofing. You will need two large baking or cookie sheets.

Makes 2 medium-sized pizzas

60 g (¼ cup) active starter

200 g (¾ cup) warm water, around 100°F (38°C)

300 g (2½ cups) strong white bread flour, plus more for dusting

4 g (½ tsp) salt, or to taste

Rice flour or ground semolina, for dusting

Toppings of your choice (I used a simple tomato sauce and sliced mozzarella)

Step 1: In a medium-sized mixing bowl, roughly mix together all the ingredients, except the rice flour or semolina and your toppings, until you have a shaggy, rough dough. Cover the bowl with a clean shower cap or your choice of cover and leave the bowl in your chosen warm spot. The dough will be sticky.

Step 2: After half an hour, perform the first set of pulls and folds by literally lifting a small handful of dough from one side of the bowl, stretching it up and across the rest of the dough. Turn the bowl slightly and repeat as many times as is necessary until the dough feels less sticky and comes together into a soft ball. This will be a warm, soft dough. Cover the bowl again and place it back in the warmth.

Step 3: After half an hour, perform the next set of pulls and folds, repeating the same actions again; the dough should be nice and stretchy and bouncy, and it should come together into a nice, smooth, soft ball. Place the covered bowl back in the warmth.

Step 4: Perform the last set of pulls and folds; the dough should come together into a nice, smooth, bouncy ball. Place the covered bowl back in the warmth for the next 3 hours, or until the dough has doubled in size.

Step 5: Once the dough is double its original size move onto the next step. Prepare your baking sheets by sprinkling them with a layer of rice flour or ground semolina.

(continued)

Same Day Sourdough Pizza (Continued)

Using a bowl scraper or your hands, gently ease the bubbly risen dough from the bowl onto a floured surface. Split the dough into two equal pieces and shape each piece into a ball. Let the balls sit on the counter for 10 minutes to rest.

After this time, place the balls on the prepared pans, and use your fingertips to push and pull the dough balls into flat rounds. I stretched mine out to 10 inches (25 cm) in diameter to make thin bases. Keep the rounds smaller for a thicker base.

Step 6: When you are ready to bake, preheat the oven to 425°F (220°C) convection or 450°F (240°C) conventional. Add your toppings to the bases and bake for 12 to 15 minutes, or 15 to 18 minutes from a cold start, or until the cheese is melted and browned and the base is cooked and crisp. Remove and serve.

Alternatively, parbake the plain bases (without toppings) to use at a later time. Bake at the directed temperatures for 10 to 15 minutes from a cold start or 5 to 10 minutes in a preheated oven depending on the thickness of your bases. Remove from the oven and allow to cool. When you are ready to use them, cover the surface of the bases with the toppings of your choice and bake at the same directed temperatures directly on the oven rack for 10 to 15 minutes, or 15 to 18 minutes from a cold start, or until browned.

Same Day Poppy Seed Sourdough Rolls

These quick and easy sourdough rolls are made using My Master Recipe (page 33) that has been converted to be able to make them within a few hours, ideal if you want rolls ready for lunch or dinner. The poppy seeds add extra flavor, but you can also make the same recipe without including them, if you choose.

TIMETABLE: To plan to make these, allow 5 to 6 hours from start to finish from the time that your starter is ready to use.

PREP: Refer to the chapter introduction on page 175 for details about how to prepare your starter for this recipe, and choosing a warm place for proofing. You will need a medium-sized baking sheet, about 10 x 14 inches (26 x 36 cm) (see Top Tip).

Makes 12 rolls

100 g (½ cup) active starter

325 g (1¼ cups) warm water, around 100°F (38°C)

500 g (4 cups) strong white bread flour, plus more for dusting

25 g (¼ cup) poppy seeds

7 g (1 tsp) salt, or to taste

Rice flour, for dusting

Step 1: In a medium-sized mixing bowl, roughly mix together all the ingredients, except the rice flour, until you have a shaggy, speckled, rough dough. Cover the bowl with a clean shower cap or your choice of cover and leave the bowl in your chosen warm spot. The dough will be sticky.

Step 2: After half an hour, perform the first set of pulls and folds by literally lifting a small handful of dough from one side of the bowl, stretching it up and across the rest of the dough. Turn the bowl slightly and repeat as many times as is necessary until the dough feels less sticky and comes together into a soft ball. This will be a warm, soft dough, textured with the poppy seeds. Cover the bowl again and place it back in the warmth.

Step 3: After half an hour, perform the next set of pulls and folds, repeating the same actions again; the dough should be nice and stretchy and bouncy, and it should come together into a nice smooth, soft ball. Place the covered bowl back in the warmth.

Step 4: Perform the last set of pulls and folds; the dough should come together into a nice, smooth, bouncy ball. Place the covered bowl back in the warmth for the next 3 hours, or until the dough has doubled in size.

Step 5: Once the dough is double its original size—it may be soft from the warm proofing, but it should not be floppy—sprinkle a layer of rice flour onto your baking sheet.

Turn the dough out onto a floured surface. Using a dough knife, cut the dough into twelve pieces, as equal as you can by eye, and shape each piece into a ball. Place the balls onto the prepared baking sheet, evenly spaced apart, cover the whole pan with a large reused plastic bag or a clean, damp tea towel, and allow them to proof again for 1½ to 2 hours.

Step 6: When you are ready to bake, decide whether you would like to bake in a preheated oven or from a cold start. If preheating, set the oven to 400°F (200°C) convection or 425°F (220°C) conventional.

Step 7: If you preheated the oven, bake the rolls uncovered for 16 to 18 minutes, or until nicely risen and starting to brown.

To bake from a cold start, place the uncovered pan of dough in the oven, set the temperature as directed and bake for a total of 18 to 20 minutes, or until nicely risen and browning.

Step 8: Once baked, remove from the oven and eat once slightly cooled.

Top Tip:

I use a medium-sized baking or cookie sheet and allow my rolls to kiss as they bake; if you would prefer your rolls not to touch, use a larger baking sheet.

Same Day Sourdough Pita Breads

Fancy some freshly baked sourdough pitas with your lunch or dinner? This recipe enables you to make them within 5 to 6 hours to be able to enjoy them fast and fresh. Eat them with dips or split and fill them with your favorite fillings.

TIMETABLE: To plan to make these, allow 5 to 6 hours from start to finish from the time that your starter is ready to use.

PREP: Refer to the chapter introduction on page 175 for details about how to prepare your starter for this recipe, and choosing a warm place for proofing. You will also need a large baking or cookie sheet.

Makes 6 pitas

60 g (¼ cup) active starter

200 g (¾ cup plus 2 tbsp) warm water, around 100°F (38°C)

10 g (1 tbsp) olive oil

300 g (2½ cups) strong white bread flour, plus more for dusting

4 g (½ tsp) salt, or to taste

Step 1: In a medium-sized mixing bowl, roughly mix together all the ingredients until you have a shaggy, rough dough. Cover the bowl with a clean shower cap or your choice of cover and leave the bowl in your chosen warm spot. The dough will be sticky.

Step 2: After half an hour, perform the first set of pulls and folds by literally lifting a small handful of dough from one side of the bowl, stretching it up and across the rest of the dough. Turn the bowl slightly and repeat as many times as is necessary until the dough feels less sticky and comes together into a soft ball. This will be a warm, soft dough, silky from the oil. Cover the bowl again and place it back in the warmth.

Step 3: After half an hour, perform the next set of pulls and folds, repeating the same actions again; the dough should be nice and stretchy and bouncy, and it should come together into a nice smooth, soft ball. Place the covered bowl back in the warmth.

Step 4: Perform the last set of pulls and folds; the dough should come together into a nice, smooth, bouncy ball. Place the covered bowl back in the warmth for the next 3 hours, or until the dough has doubled in size.

Step 5: Once the dough is double its original size—it may be soft from the warm proofing, but it should not be floppy—turn the dough out onto a floured surface. Using a dough knife, cut the dough into six pieces, as equal as you can by eye, and shape each piece into a ball. Using a rolling pin, roll each ball into a large, thin, flat circle, 4 to 5 inches (10 to 12 cm) in diameter, or a 7- or 8-inch (18- or 20-cm)-long oval.

Step 6: When you are ready to bake, decide whether you would like to bake in a preheated oven or from a cold start. If preheating, set the oven to 425°F (220°C) convection or 450°F (230°C) conventional.

Step 7: If you preheated the oven, bake uncovered for 5 minutes, or until puffed up and starting to brown slightly.

To bake from a cold start, place the baking sheet in the oven, set the temperature as directed and bake uncovered for a total of 7 minutes, or until puffed up and only slightly browning.

Step 8: Once baked, remove the bread from the oven and eat once slightly cooled.

Top Tip:
Store leftover pitas in a sealed container to keep them soft and fresh.

How to Keep a Sourdough Journal

The best way to make sourdough successfully for you, in your kitchen, is to make notes about each dough and loaf and create your very own sourdough journal; this way, you can discover your very best version of any recipe or process. By keeping a sourdough journal throughout the year, you will also be able to create a picture of how the changing seasons affect your doughs.

Recording the exact flour you used and noting the feel and texture of the dough will allow you to judge how that flour behaves. It will build the ideal picture for your sourdough-making success. This can then become a personal sourdough baking reference for you.

In this section, I have listed my recommendations for the notes to keep with each bake.

Recipe title: _____

Quantities: _____

Brand(s) of flour used: _____

Time dough was first mixed: _____

Time the dough was left to bulk proof: _____

Room temperature during the bulk proof: _____

How long the dough took to double in size: _____

How the dough felt once it had fully proofed (*for example: structured, firm, sticky, wet, sloppy?*): _____

_____

Did the dough hold its shape when it was turned out of the banneton?: _____

_____

Could you score it smoothly?: _____

How did the loaf bake?: _____

Note the external shape, how the loaf looked inside, what the texture was like (*for example: evenly spread with equally sized holes, or did the loaf have an even spread of holes, small dense holes or large uneven holes?*): _____

_____

Note how the loaf tasted and felt (*for example: perfect! Or, was it sour, not sour, light, heavy, damp, gummy?*): _____

_____

Once you have a set of notes and observations, if they are things you feel you want to work on or amend, refer to the troubleshooting pages (pages 53–58) in part I of the book to apply changes to your next bake. All possible outcomes are discussed in those pages.

Acknowledgments

My first thank-you goes to Sarah Monroe at Page Street Publishing for allowing me to write this second book about sourdough and for all of her great support and direction throughout the process. Sarah has truly made this an enjoyable and amazing journey.

My second thank-you goes to everyone on all my social media platforms for all of their interaction, support and feedback. This book, and my previous book, have only happened because of your interest and your questions, and I hope that you find everything that you read in this book to be helpful and useful in your sourdough making. You all motivate and inspire me daily.

Once again, I must thank James Kennedy for his wonderful photos and for allowing me to get involved with the food styling, for teaching me about the intricacies of food photography, for taste testing so many of my recipes and for sharing this journey with me.

Endless thank-yous to so many people for their endless support, including everyone at Matthews Cotswold Flours, especially to Bertie for teaching me even more about flour; spice boy supremo Sanjay from Spice Kitchen UK; baking equipment superstar Phil from Eco Baker; Julia from My Little Vintage; Annie Gunn Vintage for the great selection of props; and everyone at my favorite food magazine, *delicious.*

I could list so many people I would like to thank for so much, but there is not enough room in this book! But truly, thank you to everyone who has ever used my methods or baked any of my recipes, and for sharing your successes with me. It makes my heart sing to see them every time.

My biggest thank-yous always go to my most favorite people in the world, my husband and son, without whom none of this would be possible. You are both my greatest loves and the greatest supporters of everything I do. Thank you, Graham and Ben, and of course, never forgetting Bob, the dog. xxx

About the Author

Elaine Boddy is a food blogger, author, sourdough baker and teacher. Through her website, foodbod Sourdough; her first book, *Whole Grain Sourdough at Home*; and her various social media platforms, Elaine helps people all over the world daily in their pursuits of making sourdough.

Elaine's first book was chosen as one of the top 20 cookbooks of 2020 by *delicious.* magazine.

Elaine lives in the middle of the beautiful countryside in a very small village in the middle of England with her husband, son and Bob the dog.

Index